CHURCH GIVING MATTERS

Praise for
Church Giving Matters

"Many pastors face the tension between *knowing* what the Bible says about stewardship, *feeling* the struggle of an unfunded budget, and *watching* most church members choose not to participate in the offering. *Church Giving Matters* breaks through the myths that hold us back, while providing practical tools that will yield nearly immediate results."

Tim Stevens
Executive Pastor, Granger Community Church,
Author of *Vision: Lost and Found*, and blogs at
LeadingSmart.com

"Ministry is often fueled by faith and hope but, as *Church Giving Matters* warns, 'hope is not a strategy.' When dealing with the subject of money and ministry it is important to remember that *the facts* are our friends and the new realities of social media and generational giving patterns cannot be ignored. *Church Giving Matters* gives pastors and church leaders both hope *and* a strategy—backed by proven principles and practices for building a better base of giving to ministries serving Christ effectively in the 21st century."

Rev. Samuel A. Schreiner III
Lead Pastor, Noroton Presbyterian Church,
Darien, CT, and Trustee, Gordon College

"Having come through some of the most challenging economic times in recent history, churches have found ways to overcome and even thrive using many of the down-to-earth, practical approaches found in *Church Giving Matters*. For too long, our churches have taken a pass when it comes to facing the very real opportunities that exist if we simply do the work. Ben and Joel lay it out in plain English—you and I just need to put it into practice!"

Scott Anderson
Executive Pastor, Eagle Brook Church,
Twin Cities, Minnesota

"At last there is a book with page after page of instruction for church leaders on how to help others grow into joyful, purpose-filled giving. The church has needed this manual on giving. Pastors will use it to give vitality to their preaching on stewardship. Everyday believers will use it to chart a path toward a life of giving. And ministries will be funded that will change the world."

Ben Gill
Founder of RSI and Author of *The Joy of Giving*
and *Stewardship: The Biblical Basis of Living*

"In a day when budgets are tight and giving is incredibly challenging, this book is worth its weight in gold . . . if not diamonds. For every pastor, staff member, and committed lay leader, this volume is invaluable."

Dr. Jerry Sutton
Vice President of Academic Development,
Midwestern Baptist Theological Seminary, and
Author of *A Primer on Biblical Preaching*

"Every decade a stewardship resource comes along that influences positive change in giving. This book can truly 'cause' an 'effect' in your own church. Masterfully crafted advice lies within the pages of this book, which if followed, will positively impact 'what you'll have' for 'what you want to do.' This will be one of the best stewardship books, nay references, you will buy and use today! Give one to every deacon and elder in your church. I did!"

Dr. Scott Preissler
Eklund Professor of Steward Leadership,
Southwestern Baptist Theological Seminary, and
Impact Strategist for the *NIV Stewardship Study Bible*

"It's time for pastors and church leaders to approach funding in a different way. The old has gone; the new has come. Read this book!"

Patrick Johnson
Chief Architect, Generous Church,
and Co-author of *Generosity*

"There have always been a few bright individuals who could see the future. Here is an opportunity to get ahead of the curve on funding and doing more ministry."

Ashley Clayton
Associate Vice President of Stewardship, Executive
Committee of the Southern Baptist Convention

CHURCH GIVING MATTERS

More Money Really Does
Mean More Ministry

SECOND EDITION

JOEL MIKELL & BEN STROUP

To those striving to fund Kingdom ministry
and desiring a more sustainable model for ministry

+ + +

Contents

Foreword

By Joel Mikell

In March of 2010, I was visiting my dear friend Dr. Billy Compton, who at the time was executive associate for Co-operative Program and Resources at the Kentucky Baptist Convention in Louisville, Kentucky. As I was leaving his office to return to the airport, he walked over to his bookcase and handed me a book, asking if I had ever heard of a guy named Ben Stroup or if I had read his book *Church Giving Matters*. I told Billy that I did not know Ben and I had not read his book, but since it appeared to have something to do with a deep passion of mine—stewardship—I would take it and read it on one of my flights. I took the book, thanked Billy, put it in my backpack, and left for the airport.

Several weeks later on a long flight from Charlotte to Dallas, I began reading *Church Giving Matters*. What I found was an immediate resonance with Ben's beliefs and convictions about giving and biblical stewardship. I loved the fact that he was not afraid to use the word *stewardship*. I also found he was spot on in his awareness of the ever-evolving changes in our culture and the impact those changes were going to have on funding for ministry in the local church in the very near future. Finally, I discovered a refreshing boldness in Ben's challenge to pastors and church leaders to rethink and recalibrate everything they were doing in the area of stewardship in order to create a stable, sustainable source of funding for life-changing, transformational ministry. I wanted to meet this guy!

In March of 2011, I finally met Ben at the Twist Restaurant in Jackson, Tennessee. We spent several hours talking about—you guessed it—stewardship, growing joyful givers, and our mutual calling to help churches connect resources to vision. I shared with Ben my own deep convictions and passions about the steward and stewardship. I told Ben I believe that:

Stewardship is profoundly spiritual before it is financial (Psalm 24:1).

- Everything that I have—everything that I am—is a blessing and a gift from God!
- Our resources are a sacred trust—God still owns it all!

Stewardship is intimately worshipful (1 Chronicles 29:11–16).

- It is about giving God that which we deeply value—just as we offer God our praise and adoration.
- It is about commitment and re-surrender!

Stewardship is inextricably connected to our relationship with God and God's people (Matthew 28:19–20).

- Our resources of time, talent, temple, and treasure follow our relationships.
- In the local church, it is always about people, relationships, and making disciples.
- All ministry takes place in the context of relationships.

Stewardship demands accountability (Matthew 25:14–30).

- The parable of the talents—we will give an account.
- ROI—are you seeing measurable results?

Stewardship is transformational (Matthew 6:21).

- The heart of giving and stewardship is ultimately a matter of the heart.
- Giving and generosity not only changes us, it changes what we give to.

Stewardship is God's business plan for funding the ministries of the church (Matthew 6:33).

- He has already given to the church everything that is needed to accomplish what he wants accomplished in his church. God is not cheap or forgetful.

- It's never about available resources; it is always about trust and obedience to release the needed resources!

We concluded that stewardship is not as much about *activity* as it is *identity*. It is who we are! It is a lifestyle! We also agreed that stewardship is not as much about *what we do* . . . it is more about *how we live* out God's calling in our lives to be followers of Christ!

I came away from that initial meeting feeling that God, through Billy Compton, had placed that book in my hands a year earlier as a way of connecting our mutual callings and passions to help churches resource God's ministry vision for the local church.

Now a year and hundreds of conversations, e-mails, and texts later, I am incredibly delighted and humbled to be working with Ben Stroup on this updated and revised edition of *Church Giving Matters*. Any time during the reading of this book, or after you are finished, check out the bonus section at the end: 31 Practical Steps to a More Generous Church. It will help you utilize the information and inspiration you glean from each chapter.

It is our prayer and desire that within these pages you will find an appropriate balance between theology, theory, and action steps that will produce results.

Isaac Watts, in his timeless hymn "When I Survey the Wondrous Cross," reminds that sacrificial love always expresses itself in sacrificial giving. For God so loved the world that he *gave* his only Son. Christ loved us and *gave* his life for our salvation. One of the hymn's stanzas, reflecting

back on the amazing love of God through Christ, ends with
a call to a life of stewardship—of our soul, our life, our all:

> Were the whole realm of nature mine,
> That were a present far too small;
> Love so amazing, so divine,
> Demands my soul, my life, my all.

Introduction

By Ben Stroup

This week pastors are doing all the right things. They are preaching and teaching. They are visiting and reaching out to the people in their community. They are dreaming and communicating those dreams. They are working harder than they ever imagined and justifying it as the price to fulfill the call God has placed on their life, yet they feels haunted by monthly budgets and balance sheets that seem to have more influence over their decisions than prayer.

This week pastors are in meetings deciding which staff members they'll have to let go. Most of the revenue that supported the overwhelming budgets of these once thriving ministries came from investment income. There were large sums of money that their churches had collected and invested through the years—so large that there was little need to regularly ask for money to cover operational expenses. But now the market is down and business administrators say they must cut one-third of budgeted expenses—that means people and positions.

This week pastors are leading a community of aging people faced with a shrinking prospect base as the children of these members are leaving for a different place to live and work. As active members of this faith community leave this world for the next, there is no one to replace the funds provided through their generous giving. The church has always been able to pay the bills and survive. But now people are losing the battle with cancer—members who represent half of the largest, most faithful givers in their church.

This week a pastor learned that an abortion clinic is scheduled to be built just a few miles from the church. Church leaders have a vision for a pregnancy counseling center in the vacant building just opposite of the chosen abortion clinic site. They quickly call an informal finance committee meeting to share ideas. Unfortunately, the chairman doesn't think the church has the money to even consider the program and strongly cautions the pastor that moving in this direction could jeopardize the church's ability to pay salaries.

Somewhere pastors are waking up knowing this will be the last time they make the drive to the office as they know it. This will be the last day they turn the key to their church building, preach from their pulpit, offer an invitation at the end of their message, and baptize in their baptistry. This week their churches will be auctioned off to the highest bidders. Every time they drive by their building, the echo of their hopes and dreams will rush to the center of their mind and a sense of loss will surely follow. Their lips will quiver and their voices shake for months, perhaps years, as they try to articulate how things completely fell apart.

Each of these real-life scenarios leave pastors feeling overwhelmed and underprepared. My guess is that while you may not have been through a situation as dramatic as those described above, there has been a time in your ministry, perhaps multiple times, when you felt inspired by God but were restricted by the resources available to you and your church to accomplish those dreams.

It's not your fault. You probably didn't cover this in seminary. In fact, you likely graduated with the hopes that your ability to parse the Greek and Hebrew languages and craft meaningful sermons would ensure that you would be able to avoid most conversations related to money and giving and financial solvency. But you soon realized—just weeks into your first pastorate—that you were being measured not by your theological prowess but by the dollars in the plate and the people in the pews.

All pastors have had that epiphany when they realize what they thought they were called to do came with a hidden responsibility they didn't expect. There is perhaps no greater calling than to lead a local church. The church is the primary unit God has designed and empowered to carry forward the earthly ministry of Christ until his ultimate return. There is no plan B. God didn't leave us with a backup plan. Therefore, complete failure is not an option.

> Nowhere in anyone's call to ministry is there any mention of the ministry of money, yet that seems to be the very thing that drives every decision.

Yet this hidden responsibility scares most people who are drawn to positions of ministry leadership because it involves money, a subject that has been the bane of so many in such a public profession. Nowhere in anyone's call to ministry is there any mention of the ministry of money, yet that seems to be the very thing that drives every decision. It's always lurking in the corner of the minds of those involved in both the strategic ministry planning process and the execution of that plan: will there be enough money to really do this?

If you have ever felt like no one bothered to show you the fine print before you signed the contract and agreed to lead a local church, then these words and sentences and pages are for you. If you have ever questioned why biblical expository preaching, faithful home and hospital visits, and consistent outreach programs aren't enough to generate the funds necessary to accomplish the ministry God has placed on your heart, then these words and sentences and pages are for you. If you have ever felt frustrated in affecting change and fully funding the ministry budgets you propose, then these words and sentences and pages are for you.

This book is not the end all or be all. Rather, it begins a vital conversation that speaks to the heart of the local church's ability to bring into reality the ministry God has called them to do. This book is not about how to afford fancy suits, shiny new shoes, brand-new cars, or expensive houses. That's another book, and there are plenty of them. This book was written because I couldn't find the book I needed while pastoring a small, rural congregation of people grappling with a changing community and the need to build a more sustainable funding model to ensure the ministry of this church continued long after the faithful few passed from this world to the next. And now, for this second edition, I'm honored to partner with Joel Mikell, as we dig deeper into this reality: More money really does mean more ministry.

Each chapter is designed to give you the tools you need in vocabulary, theory, and practice to begin. It's important to remember that context matters. Not every congregation is the same; not every community is the same. The broad application of a successful model breaks down when different churches in different communities attempt to reproduce the same results in the same way.

Here is an overview of each chapter:

Chapter 1—Funding: The Fuel for Ministry. In this chapter we will explore assumptions about money and local church ministry so as to provide a context and lens through which this conversation can be interpreted and find a healthy place within the role of local church ministry leadership. A clear set of expectations will be outlined, and we will discuss how this material fits within local church ministry and pastoral leadership.

Chapter 2—Sustainability: Something Every Pastor Should Consider. Here we will discuss why being a pastor means balancing the role of shepherd with the role of organizational manager. We are most familiar with the former and often oblivious to the latter.

Chapter 3—Engagement: The Rules Have Changed. This chapter will review why the conversation has changed and how the power has shifted from the pulpit to the pew. This chapter will offer some insight into how churches have become "one more option" in the midst of a growing number of nonprofits working to gain every dollar possible from the person in the pew and why the person in the pew sees little—if any—difference between giving to a traditional nonprofit and giving to the church.

Chapter 4—Responsibility: What You Wished They Had Prepared You for in Seminary. In this section, you will discover some guiding principles to use as you form your own contextualized approach to sustainable funding models for the churches you lead. This chapter will offer some practical advice as to how to alter your approach in light of the discoveries found in the previous chapter.

Chapter 5—Transformation: Why Hope Is Not a Strategy. Finally, in this chapter we will challenge you to see stewardship as the key to the ever-increasing demand for more ministry. We will revisit why stewardship must be incorporated into every ministry plan and how it must become the catalyst for change.

The growing complexity of local church ministry is demanding more money while the rules of funding ministry are changing. It's the responsibility of pastors to strategically evaluate and implement a plan to ensure funding exists to fulfill the ministry God has placed on their hearts. My prayer is that by the end of this book, you'll feel empowered to boldly lead your church to fully funded ministry budgets and long-term sustainable ministry. The ministry of the local church and its ability to fulfill the Great Commission depend upon it.

Chapter 1

+ + +

FUNDING:
THE FUEL FOR MINISTRY

"At least one out of five American Christians—
20 percent of all US Christians—gives literally nothing
to church, parachurch, or nonreligious charities."
—*MICHAEL O. EMERSON AND CHRISTIAN SMITH*

A few words as we begin . . . Tithing and church giving have become somewhat of a political debate among the Christian community. Is tithing mandated, or is freewill giving biblically accurate? How much influence does the Old Testament have on the New Testament church? We want to settle this debate up front: We don't care.

Such conversation may be great in the halls of academia and very appropriate in settings where pastors want to manipulate theoretical precepts to support their points of view and show off in front of their peers. However, this type of activity doesn't produce results. Pastors have great responsibility; they are responsible for the financial integrity as well as the spiritual vitality of the organizations they lead.

If you're turned off or offended by what you've just read, then please don't read any further. If you're looking for a book that is full of theological vocabulary and requires a dictionary and thesaurus to be kept close by, then this book is not for you. If you're looking for an easy, quick fix, then this book is not for you.

If, however, you feel the pressure of money and ministry and feel overwhelmed, underprepared, and uncomfortable with this tension, keep reading. If you want to gain a better understanding of how to lead your church through tough and prosperous economic times, then keep reading. If you believe God has provided all the resources you need to accomplish the ministry He has placed in your heart, then keep reading.

What We Believe

We believe the church is the primary institution empowered by God at Pentecost to carry forward the work of the Great Commission until his ultimate return. Because we believe that, we are committed to supporting the work of the local church, not denominations. Some have put the proverbial cart before the horse. The local church does not exist to support the work of the denomination. Rather, the denomination exists to support the work of the local church.

We believe that pastors are the primary conduits to fully

funded budgets and long-term sustainable ministry. Money is not the end that justifies the means. Money is merely the fuel that ensures the work continues until Christ returns. Our conversations about money and the church typically are the result of capital campaigns. A great deal of literature already exists on this subject. While it can be an element of a sustainable ministry, the purpose of this book is much broader than how a church can better raise funds to build a building.

We believe sustainable funding models for ministry will look and feel different in every church. The important task of pastors is to inform themselves on the strategies and tools available to be able to make critical decisions that result in the necessary funding for ministry. We also believe that creating a strategy and plan for sustainable funding is a dynamic process. It's something that must be revisited every time a pivotal leadership decision is made and upon completion of every ministry program or event. Building a habit of measuring effectiveness will ensure that your members see a connection between their giving and the ministry of your church.

> Money is not the end that justifies the means. Money is merely the fuel that ensures the work continues until Christ returns.

The conversation on stewardship and giving has been a marginal one for far too long. It's time to shift the conversation from "What do we have to cut survive?" to "What does God want us to do next?" This subtle shift changes our perspective and helps encourage us to see the opportunities available to us rather than the limitations that restrict us.

This book is only the beginning. By design, it will not answer—or even attempt to address—all relevant questions. Our hope is that it will facilitate a conversation that is taking place across the landscape of churches everywhere: how can I better fund the ministry God has called me to accomplish? We do not hesitate to proclaim that God will provide, but those faced with seemingly impossible circumstances quietly wonder to themselves if God will come through again.

Let's Be Honest

Money makes pastors sweat. It increases their heart rates and causes them to shift in their seats. Few pastors considered their calling would include the ministry of money. We suspect that if most pastors had a hint of the reality check that comes in the first few months of their first pastorate, some might have made a different decision.

There is so much anxiety surrounding money, its misuse, and the perception of power it brings that it is often left alone for fear of not knowing exactly what to do or say. This unfortunate reality has produced a void of teaching and preaching on the subject, which has resulted in an entire generation of Christians who are slow to make the connection that confessing Jesus as Lord means he owns everything and expects us to manage the resources he has provided to the advancement of the Kingdom, not our personal agendas.

The annual stewardship campaign is as painful for the pastor to preach as it is for the person in the pew to hear. It's not for the lack of good resources or biblical substance. Rather, this directly stems from leaving stewardship out of pastor training and church strategy planning. Something has to change. It's time to drop the pretense and the pseudo-theological vocabulary and just be honest with people—especially the people in our pews—when it comes to church giving.

Seven Things You Need to Know

Each of these is important and provides a basis for the remainder of this book. These basic premises provide insight into our assumptions about money and local church ministry. It's not necessary that you agree with all of them, only that you keep these in mind as we move forward.

1. The church is a nonprofit organization that exists only through the donations of people.

Strip away the things that are specific to churches and what you are left with is an organization of people designed to accomplish a specific work that provides its membership with opportunities for leadership and community service. All of this is funded through the contributions of those who believe in the cause and goals that this organization upholds and affirms.

Our point is not to strip away all the mystery and theology that are intricately connected with the makeup of the church; we want you to better understand why your church should be as concerned with sustainable funding levels as is the executive director of the local nonprofit. As the demands upon churches become more complex, the funding necessary to meet those demands increases. Every nonprofit is faced with this reality. Pastors and church leaders are fooling themselves if they believe that they can avoid this certain reality.

2. The habits of giving begin with the worldview of the giver.

Church leaders should be focused on creating a culture of generosity. Pounding the pulpit is quickly fading as a trusted strategy to increase giving in your church. Generosity is a spiritual characteristic and begins with a biblical understanding of the Lordship of Christ.

America is built upon the desire to be free of obligation to someone else. This directly contradicts our belief that what we have is God's and is freely given to us to use to build up and benefit the work of the Kingdom. Knowing this helps inform church leaders and shape their strategies to begin initiating a change in the way their membership views giving and the role it plays within the life of a believer.

3. Churches have an advantage over every other nonprofit.

A traditional nonprofit spends a great deal of money each year to promote its mission and ask for monetary support to fund that mission. No other nonprofit is provided with a built-in, weekly donor cultivation event called weekly worship services; churches are. But churches don't understand how to use those opportunities to reinforce their mission and solidify consistent giving from their membership.

Churches are best positioned to capture the greatest percentage of dollars available from every member. It's up to us to take advantage of the opportunity and channels we have been given to ensure fully funded budgets and long-term sustainable ministry.

4. Churches are the worst at capturing the dollar.

Church leaders too often rely on pseudo-theological vocabulary or other empty rhetoric that sounds good but delivers no "call to action" that results in consistent giving behavior. Churches need to shift their focus to demonstrating the ministry impact of every dollar. This is why so many Christians can justify sending their tithe—in portion or in full—to parachurch and other nonprofits that are much better at demonstrating what every dollar accomplishes.

Leadership will need to make a shift in seeing their members as shareholders. Shareholders are all owners of a public company, and public companies make decisions based on how those decisions will impact the value of the shareholders' stakes in the business. We're not proposing that we sell our churches on the open market. We are advocating that we adopt some of the reporting mechanisms that public companies use to demonstrate the progress they are making in the marketplace and document each success. People want to know you know what you're doing with the money they contribute.

5. Churches that avoid talking about biblical stewardship risk losing it all.

If churches continue to be silent in the area of biblical stewardship—our time, talent, and treasures—the number of volunteers, the lay leadership, and the giving levels needed to operate and grow a complex organization such as the church will cease to exist. Stewardship for many is an "old" word that has no place in the modern Christian's vocabulary. If truth be known, many of us would admit that our training in this area has been very limited, so we base our perceptions on our experience: the annual stewardship emphasis and the occasional capital campaign. But stewardship is so much more, and we believe people who cite Christianity as shallow are not being challenged to see how to integrate their faith in a holistic way where everything they have is to be given as an offering to the source of all our gifts.

We would suggest that stewardship is less scary for the person in the pew than the person in the pulpit might think. It has been our experience that people are looking for a vocabulary and discipline to measure their use of God's gifts to the advancement of the Gospel and the fulfillment of the Great Commission. However, our silence has left them to put the pieces together themselves—a dangerous proposition indeed.

6. Giving levels and habits should be seen as measurement tools.

Giving is an outward sign of an inward commitment. If people have a hard time giving money to your church, then they aren't fully committed. Knowing this leads to much deeper, more comprehensive conversations that could reveal some important information about your congregation.

Most of the people leading stewardship committees today are already faithful givers. They can't imagine and understand why everyone else doesn't think and give like they do. The reality is that most of your membership doesn't contribute a dime to your church. There is a great opportunity to grow your giving base, but that opportunity has to be cultivated and nurtured until the response is nothing less than generous.

7. Church giving is connected to your ministry plan.

What's your vision? Is it big enough to inspire someone else? If not, dream bigger. People want to give to causes that they believe in because they want to accomplish something larger than they could through their own efforts. If people can accomplish what you provide through your ministry on their own, they will and they'll take their tithe with them.

People have an internal compass that we in the church call the Holy Spirit. This compass drives people to a place where they want more than they currently have.

They want to be a part of something that provides a lasting impression on the world around them. If your church isn't giving them something to talk about other than the next fellowship dinner, chances are they'll find a church that has fully embraced a missional mindset and is practicing their faith through its ministry plan.

Stop using failed persuasive techniques and start inspiring a generous culture. It will change your life, your ministry, and your church. And you will have more money for more ministry.

Three Brutal Facts About Giving

The Pareto Principle is more commonly known as the 80/20 rule. In other words, 80 percent of your ministry is driven by 20 percent of your membership. The same is true with respect to church giving habits too. Twenty percent of your congregation is giving 80 percent of your total budgeted funds. This will either paralyze you or motivate you to become more strategic.

The 20 percent are the ones who end up on stewardship and finance committees. These leaders can't imagine or understand why 80 percent of the congregation doesn't give. What we've found to be true is that often the 20 percent think they are actually representing 40 or 50 percent of the congregation. Most church leaders think their church is different (i.e., better) than the average. When they complete a church giving profile, this group is consistently surprised to learn that their church is just like every other church in that there are a small number of faithful givers giving a majority of the budgeted funds.

> While years are spent preparing pastors to preach, without a consistent stewardship education program pastors won't have a pulpit to preach from.

Here are the brutal facts:

1. When your long-term funding strategy is hung on the giving habits of a small percentage of your entire congregation, you are tempting fate. Someone in that small group will leave the church, change jobs, lose his or her job, die, etc. If you're not building giving habits with the 80 percent group, you are leaving yourself wide open for disaster to happen.

2. Providing things like electronic giving and offering envelopes are designed to encourage giving among the 80 percent—the largest body of your giving base. These systematic tools are not designed for the small group of faithful givers in your church. These tools give you the opportunity to grow your giving base, which makes you more likely to sustain a change in economic conditions and support a growth in the ministry activities of your church.

3. *Stewardship is more important than your sermon preparation.* (We're anticipating some negative feedback for this one. Before you burn this book, hear us out.) Stewardship is about discipleship. It speaks to giving of ourselves—our time, talent, and treasure—because we recognize that everything we have is from God and is designed to be used to multiply Kingdom efforts.

While years are spent preparing pastors to preach, without a consistent stewardship education program pastors won't have a pulpit to preach from. (Note: Pulpit can be symbolic if you are naturally opposed to the piece of furniture that is usually found center stage at traditional churches.)

Now more than ever pastors and church leaders must concern themselves with the fundamentals of organizational funding, stability, and sustainability. Let us sum it up by saying this: More Money = More Ministry. No Money = No Ministry. Those are the brutal facts.

Tithing Outside the Church

There are some definite shifts taking place in the minds of American Christians related to tithing. Integrating these shifts into your overall funding strategy will be critical to your ability to remain financially solvent. Two significant ones are:

A growing number of Christians no longer believe the tithe is solely reserved for the church. More and more Christians are finding themselves dividing their 10 percent among their local church and other noble charitable endeavors. There is no regret or remorse. Gone are the days when church leaders could assume that the tithe of every Christian would find its way into the church offering plate each week. As the culture demands more transparency from the organizations they financially support as consumers, this sentiment is translated into the church context too. The general nonprofit world is already grappling with this reality; the church isn't exempt from it either.

Christians want their tithes to count in measurable ways. Churches in the not so near future—maybe even today (or yesterday)—will be required to document the ministry results supported by the tithes and offerings received from their membership base. The luster of undesignated funds is diminishing. American Christians want to know where their money is going, how it's being used, and the impact it's making.

The end result of these shifts is that the church is becoming one of many charitable giving options instead of the central or primary charitable giving option for many American Christians. The control is shifting back to the person in the pew. No longer can church leaders sit back and expect the tradition of tithing to the local church to dictate how Christians give back to God. The new era of giving for American Christians doesn't exclude churches from the mix of charitable giving opportunities, but it requires the church to make a case for why it should be the recipient of those funds.

It's Not About You

There is a revolution taking place. Social media tools are returning the power back to the individual from the institution. There was a time when the institution controlled the message. Now it matters more what others are saying about the organization than what the organization is saying about itself. For those who still believe in the old model of communication, they risk losing credibility by continuing to resist this irreversible change.

What does that mean for those of us concerned with stewardship and giving in the church? It doesn't mean that church leaders should begin to view members as consumers. We've been down that road, and it's disastrous for everyone involved. Here's what we think it means: what's relevant, helpful, insightful, etc., is determined by the person in the pew instead of the voice from the pulpit. We must give up our top-down mentality. This is exactly what made Jesus so successful at influencing people. (Of course, it's also what led to his death.)

If we are going to be successful at reseeding the conversation on stewardship and giving and capturing more money for more ministry, it's going to have to be a movement that begins with the church member instead of the pastor or other staff members. When was the last time we made a case for biblical stewardship that compelled the person in the pew through story and life transformation rather than expository preaching and rational argumentation. If we don't, someone else will. And the chance that the one who will do this successfully will be outside the church is very high.

It's time to get our game on. Are you ready to lose control and inspire others to multiply your ministry? No one is waiting to hear what the organization has to say. What pockets of people are waiting for is to hear what the people in your pews are saying about you.

Is Focusing on Money Even Christian?

We think there are many pastors and church leaders who believe that any conversation about money or fund-raising is nothing better than a four-letter word that should be forbidden from the Christian's vocabulary. It feels dirty, and it's more dreaded than getting all your teeth pulled at the same time.

In conversations with some pastors, they say that fund-raising isn't something that should concern a minister. The money needed will be provided "by the work of the Spirit." That sounds very pastoral, but it doesn't work. It's the equivalent of CEOs saying that customers who buy products or services need the CEOs and companies more than the companies and CEOs need their customers. That's simply not true.

We're not diminishing the role of the Holy Spirit in the

work of the church. It's central to our effectiveness in bringing about the Kingdom of God on earth. But when we take that reality and use that as an excuse as to why we're not responsible or shouldn't be held accountable for the results we produce, we misuse theology to justify our own interests and cover up our own insecurities.

Stewardship and giving are central to the mission and viability of the church as an organization. If there is no money for ministry, then there is no ministry. The church has operational needs, and ministry costs money. So church giving is not just central to the life of the believer, it should be at the top of every church leader's list.

No one is asking you to become a money expert or assume the persona of a nonprofit development officer. But as the spiritual leader of your church, it's imperative that you know enough to ensure your church is healthy on all fronts—particularly when it relates to a subject like funding, which is the fuel for your ministry.

DISCUSSION QUESTIONS

1. What assumptions did you have about money when you first started out? How have they changed between then and now?

2. Are the stewardship practices of your church producing the results you desire? Why or why not?

3. Which of the "Seven Things You Need to Know" did you *not* know (or choose to ignore) before reading them?

4. How can you keep your church from becoming just one of many charitable giving opportunities available to them?

5. When it comes to talking about giving, are you speaking the language of your members (ministry relevance and impact) or do they only hear of the church's needs (budgets and expenses)?

Chapter 2

+ + +

SUSTAINABILITY: SOMETHING EVERY PASTOR SHOULD CONSIDER

". . . Both for-profits and nonprofits must address
[sustainable funding] to effectively
carry out their missions."
—TOM RALSER

What is sustainability? Sustainability is defined by Merriam-Webster's dictionary as being "a method of harvesting or using a resource so that the resource is not depleted or permanently damaged." The last chapter focused on answering the questions related to why funding fuels our ministry and what should be the posture of church leaders and pastors related to money and ministry.

Sustainability is not a topic of conversation that is widely discussed in thriving economic times. When we find ourselves in a strong economic climate, the focus tends to be on models for growth. Sustaining something is hardly as exciting as growing something. Nonetheless, it should be of utmost importance to the pastor in both good and bad economic times.

This is true in our personal financial situations as well as our organizational situations. We haven't met one personal money management expert to date who does not encourage people to establish an emergency fund. Why is this such an important step to financial independence? Times of growth will become times of decline, and times of decline will become times of growth. High school business teachers drill into their students' heads that there are only two things you need to know about economics: 1) there is no such thing as a free lunch, and 2) what goes up will come down.

As churches have exponentially increased in size and complexity, more and more congregations are discovering that weekly contributions aren't enough to hedge against the unexpected.

There will be times when a deficit is created between income and expenses due to unforeseen or unexpected circumstances. Having an emergency fund provides a way for you to remain financially solvent even when your expenses exceed your income. This is true in a church context too. The conversation on sustainability within the context of church management ensures that the organization remains solvent when one or more funding streams are unexpectedly disrupted.

Era of Easy Money Ends for Churches

There was a day and time when churches could operate from one stream of income: weekly contributions from their membership. With little to no debt and with a small volunteer or bivocational staff, many churches had little concern over things like sustainability. When the unexpected occurred, someone would step in and provide the funds necessary to cover the expense. As churches have exponentially increased in size and complexity, more and more congregations are discovering that weekly contributions aren't enough to hedge against the unexpected.

The practice of charitable giving has always been a habit that churches depended upon. The assumption has been held for as long as either of us can remember, that if you have enough people attending and participating in the ministry of your church, you'll have all the money you ever need. That theory breaks down when the people you are counting on to give run out of money too.

If your church is operating off one stream of income, such as weekly contributions or investment income, you are leaving your church in a very vulnerable position. And if the worst case scenario does happen, you may not be able to recover. The most tangible examples of what can happen to a church when the unexpected happens can be found in capital improvement ventures.

As our nation is still feeling tremors of the current economic crisis, churches that borrowed money to buy and build bigger buildings are finding themselves in some very difficult situations. These churches entered into these agreements with the best of intentions. Behind every doubt was the sentiment: if you build it, they will come. But what happens when they don't come? What happens when they do come, but they have no money to bring along with them? It's simple. When you borrow money to build a building and don't have enough to pay it back, you will find yourself involved in what is known as foreclosure.

What does it say about a church that is forced to seek bankruptcy protection because it can no longer afford the building payments? What impact does it have on the pastor and the members who thought they did all the right things, prayed all the right prayers, asked all the right questions, yet still ended up defeated and discouraged?

Please hear us when we say this: capital investments are not the problem. The churches that will most likely find themselves in the situation described above are the victims of the absence of a sustainability strategy. So when weekly contributions dropped (contributions they assumed would stay the same . . . forever!), they were no longer able to make the payments and support the other core operational expenses necessary to operate the building. No one could have anticipated it, but at the end of the day, the pastor is the individual ultimately responsible for the situation.

The Pastor Is a Shepherd and an Organizational Manager

The more time we spend with pastors, the more apparent it becomes that many do not separate their role as shepherd from their role as an organizational manager. In fact, most wouldn't even think to consider themselves in such a way.

The role of pastors is complex, one in which they function in three main capacities: prophet, priest, and pastor. The role of the prophet is primarily executed through preaching and teaching. This role is well defined. The role of the priest is primarily executed through special events such as weddings, funerals, baby dedications, the Lord's Supper, baptism, etc. A secondary function of this role can be found through the practice of spiritual formation as pastors lead their congregation not only to new faith but also to a deeper faith. This is also well defined. It's not until we come to the role of pastor that we enter unknown territory for most who find themselves in positions of ministry leadership.

It has been said by one or two people that the role of the pastor is much like that of a shepherd. The shepherd is responsible for overseeing the sheep, providing food and shelter for the sheep, and ensuring the sheep are protected from unanticipated challenges that may threaten their lives. This is a perfect image of what organizational managers do. They are responsible for the operations of their organization, providing the resources necessary to operate their organizations, and anticipating unlikely scenarios to ensure viability during difficult times.

Pastor must remember that while they are called to function in the traditional roles of priest and prophet, they are also pastor, the leader of a complex (complexity and size are not necessarily related) organization of people that must be inspired to make commitments of time, talent, and treasures. Organizational managers are focused on making connections with people, driving programs and activities that embody the values of organizations, and ultimately ensure fully funded budgets and long-term sustainable ministry.

If this sounds overwhelming, that's because it is. Serving in the leadership of a local church is no different from the role of an executive director of a nonprofit organization. You have a board to which you must answer regarding organizational development and oversight; you have budgets to prepare and financial statements to interpret; you have volunteers to recruit, develop, and manage; you have community awareness goals that you'll accomplish through direct mail, special events, and sponsorships; you have programs to dream, develop, and execute; you have presentations and speeches to make at various times and in front of various audiences; and you have the responsibility to cultivate and generate the funds necessary to accomplish the goals you and the board have set.

It is little wonder that so many pastors graduate from seminary with good intentions and leave the pastorate—or worse—refuse to serve after watching others struggle to survive in the midst of what seems like a never-ending battle against limited resources such as time, talent, and money. This is an underdeveloped skill set that is an absolutely vital aspect of what it means to pastor a church.

Church Givers Expect Ministry to Continue in Good and Bad Times

Ministry is a 24/7 endeavor. There is never a time when need is not present and the expectation of the church to meet those needs is absent. These elements combine to create the perfect storm of expectation that offers little reprieve for the pastor.

Little conversation is needed regarding sustainability in good times; it's the bad times that seem to leave us anxious at the intersection of need and resources. The important thing to remember is this: silence is not an option. Ignoring the economy could prove to be a costly decision, so start talking.

> What you fear talking about the most, the people in your pews already know with certainty.

The people in your pews already know when the economy is not good; they are feeling the pressure at work, at home, from their financial planner, etc. Maybe it's time to take the lead and tell your people how it's directly impacting your church. Use this as an opportunity to recast your vision and quantify the ministry impact of your church upon your community. People appreciate honesty. And we're quite certain that the people in your pews want to see that you're thinking as carefully about church finances as they are about their personal finances. In fact, if you'll be brave enough to let them in, they'll listen. (We promise.)

Here is the irony of the situation. What you fear talking about the most, the people in your pews already know with certainty. They're just not sure you understand. And until they know you understand, they will not be as generous as they could be.

People will always have discretionary income. While they might be more careful with how they use it, they are going to give it to somebody. Why not your church? As church leaders, it's our responsibility to ensure the long-term viability of the organizations we manage that ultimately facilitate the ministry to which we are called.

Contributions Down? Time to Innovate

Nonprofits depend upon the generosity of others to fund their budgets; the church is no different. Why does it seem like we resolve year after year to "wait and see" just how strong or weak the economy will be and what impact it will have on church giving? As churches become more complex in an attempt to meet even more complex ministry needs, it's a perfect time to begin to talk about things like innovation. We predict that churches will need to become much more intentional about how they spend their money to ensure every dollar received is maximized for ministry. Innovation usually comes out of necessity.

When you experience a decline in contributions, you can either: sit in a corner and cry about it or innovate and rely on creative solutions to meet the present needs. Our hope is that churches would choose the latter rather than the former. Innovation is a big, scary word for some. Innovation has also been one of those buzzwords that the church leadership movement has borrowed from the business world and used so much that it has lost some of its appeal.

But innovation is important. In times when it's more important than ever to demonstrate what every dollar received is accomplishing by measuring ministry results, it's time to consider new ways, better ways to yield the same if not greater results. We wonder what vital ministries are on the proverbial chopping block that could be maintained, dare we suggest strengthened, with a simple touch of innovation.

Even if your contributions are down, the need is the same if not more. So get up, dry your eyes, and start thinking about new ways to multiply your ministry. Our guess is that the same Spirit that inspires leaders to innovate will also ignite the giving of your membership.

Everything Is Always on the Table

Wherever the conversation of sustainability is taking place, the necessity of evaluation is also present. Everything a church does, every program it creates, every ministry it conducts, should be carefully evaluated in light of its success or failure to determine whether it is or is not the best use of available resources.

People want to know how their money is being used and what type of impact it is making. Churches need to begin evaluating their investments by asking if each program or ministry is surrounded with excitement and participation, encouraging the spiritual growth of the believer, producing measurable results (aka impacting the Kingdom), and leading to new ministry opportunities.

People in the pew know that they have the ability to make an international impact even with a small amount of money. And people want to be inspired and encouraged that their donations—however small or large—are making a measurable impact.

Most nonprofits, knowing they are supported by a donor base, must give continual feedback as to their ability to accomplish their intended work with the donations given. This affirms the work of the nonprofit itself and ensures that those providing the donations deem the organization and its work worthy.

> What if the assumption or posture of the church leader changed from "We expect you to tithe" to "How can I show you that investing in this ministry is your best charitable giving option"?

What if the assumption or posture of the church leader changed from "We expect you to tithe" to "How can I show you that investing in this ministry is your best charitable giving option"? We know it's a radical departure from the tried-and-true methods of church funding, but we must be willing to look at this absolutely critical issue from every angle to learn what it will take to continue to build up the church—God's designed and desired vehicle for ministry on earth.

As a pastor you may find yourself repeating the phrase "Everything is always on the table" over and over again before your lay leadership team begins to naturally evaluate everything you do and determine whether it is a success or not. In order to provide a process for sustainability, there will always need to be an assumption that what is done today may or may not be done tomorrow.

Tread Carefully When Cutting Expenses

The traditional nonprofit management reaction when contributions fall below expectations is to make expense cuts. If the only way to maintain solvency as an organization is to have these conversations and make these decisions, then our advice is to tread carefully to ensure your expense cutting doesn't alienate a segment of your giving base.

Some consumers purchase products from vendors who support certain causes such as breast cancer or heart disease. Research is available that demonstrates when consumers have a choice, they are most likely to choose the brand that made a connection with a cause that served the greater good. I (Ben) find evidence of this in my own life. I recently purchased a handheld gaming system that supported breast cancer research. The brand connection made the purchasing decision easy, made me feel as if I had found exactly what I wanted at a good price, and reinforced my decision by providing me with the opportunity to support the work of a cause that's important to me.

Looking at such an experience, here is what captures our imagination: as churches project their collections and set operational budgets based on those projections, it seems prudent to evaluate any necessary cuts through the eyes of the church giver and not simply the business administrator.

If the general public is more likely to purchase a product because of its link to a cause they feel is important or connects on an emotional level, why would we expect the people in our pews to be any different? People give to their church because they connect with and support its ministry goals. If in the midst of often necessary expense cuts a program or ministry one church giver feels important is cut, this could unintentionally sever the emotional connection that initiated the giving in the first place.

Churches that wish to maintain the financial integrity

of their operations must evaluate every decision from two vantage points: the impact on the budget and how essential this program or ministry is to the larger vision of the church. (One might add that if a ministry or program is determined as nonessential and is cut and is never missed, perhaps it wasn't a good investment initially.)

Expense cuts seem to be the first solution proposed when contributions take a dip, but churches run a dangerous risk in the midst of making those decisions of cutting a program or ministry that the people in the pews see as essential. (The perception of the person in the pew matters more than church leaders care to admit.) While expense cuts do provide an immediate, short-term solution, losing the ministry connection with the person in the pew in an attempt to provide an immediate solution may actually create a long-term problem.

Suggestions for Navigating the Waters of Sustainability

The greatest risk when implementing a sustainable strategy is that we forget the inherent advantages a church has in its ability to inspire change and overcome seemingly insurmountable odds. Here are a few things to keep in mind:

1. Church attendance increases in tough times. History demonstrates that people find their way to places of worship when life throws them into unexpected and overwhelming circumstances. Capitalize on the opportunity to inspire new or less-than-regular attenders with compelling stories that connect with people on a personal and emotional level.

2. Celebrate your success. If you don't talk about your success, no one else will. Keeping people connected to the cause or organization they support is absolutely essential to building long-term, sustainable funding. Most people don't interface with your church as much as the pastor does. Find ways to encourage your membership and thank them for their support.

3. Name your strengths and use them to your advantage. When it comes to funding models, the church makes the rest of the nonprofit world jealous. Every week, church leaders are able to get in front of their membership, which reminds people of the work they are supporting and why they chose your church in the first place. The church also offers opportunities to give more consistently because you are in front of your membership more regularly than traditional nonprofits. Monthly giving is an undervalued habit to encourage with simple tools like an offering envelope service.

4. Use technology to your advantage. Begin exploring ways to connect with your membership using social media tools and through devices such as cell phones. The revolution is taking place right now: either you will roll with it or be left behind. It's time to begin cultivating relationships with a new generation of donors—a generation of people who are ready to give but who don't automatically assume the church is the best place for their dollar. It's your responsibility to demonstrate why they should give to your church.

5. *What goes down must come up.* Remember that phrase from the King James version of the Bible: "this too shall pass"? It's true. Just because you may see a temporary drop in giving doesn't mean you need to panic. Use it as an opportunity to evaluate every area of your ministry, and take the steps necessary to bring your ministry and budget in harmony with one another. (This is what you're asking of your membership as you invite them to reduce their personal debt so that they can be free to be generous givers. Why shouldn't we expect the same from ourselves?)

Stewardship may be the most unusual place for church leaders to look for encouragement in tough economic times. But these five things remind us that we have a lot to celebrate as Christians and every reason to believe the church will continue to survive and thrive just as it has for thousands of years.

The Secret to Sustainable Ministry

The role of the pastor is complex, and many never dreamed that being an organizational manager was part of the job description. The resources and people are available for you to build a sustainable organization in the midst of any economic condition. There isn't one thing, one secret that will ensure your organization will be sustainable. It's really a combination of multiple channels of contribution, maintaining focus and developing programs, and people who are inspired by and committed to your church and constantly evaluating every investment of time, talent, or treasure to ensure you are making the most of every available dollar.

There is a correlation between sustainability and endurance. An endurance athlete trains to maintain a certain level of effort over an extended period of time. Doing this well requires the athlete to eat appropriately, sleep consistently, and train strategically. It is no different for the pastor. You have been charged with managing a complex organization that will need funding, people, and programs to accomplish the goals and objectives you have set. And this must be done in good economic times and bad.

If there is one secret to endurance sports or pastoring a church, it's this: keep going. As Paul said in 1 Corinthians 9:24, "Do you not know that runners in a stadium all race, but only one receives the prize? Run in such a way that you may win."

DISCUSSION QUESTIONS

1. If one or more of your funding streams was unexpectedly disrupted (by subtraction of members or addition of expenses), how many weeks or months could the church remain solvent while maintaining its current level of ministry?

2. In the past, when contributions were down, did you go into panic mode or did you innovate? What steps did you take? What should you have done or not done?

3. Are all ministries "on the table"? Are there any that need to be evaluated more closely and, perhaps, abandoned for others?

4. Which ministries are a direct reflection of your members' hearts and your church's core mission?

5. Which of the five suggestions for navigating the waters of sustainability do you need to remind yourself of right now? How can you communicate them to your congregation?

+ + +

Chapter 3

ENGAGEMENT: THE RULES HAVE CHANGED

"People no longer give to the church simply because it is the church. The church must prove it is worthy of donations through the mark it leaves on the world."
—GEORGE BARNA

The way we communicate with one another is changing. Organizations are losing control. No longer can senior-level management contain public relations nightmares until all the details are assembled and a corporate response announced. With social media tools such as Twitter, every employee is now a spokesperson for the company. In the same way, the power of cell phones to be able to take pictures and video and e-mail that information to millions of people in a matter of minutes has created a culture of citizen journalists.

The thought of having to use a rotary dial phone or write a handwritten letter to someone, place a stamp on an envelope, and drop it by the post office just won't satisfy our incessant need for more and more, faster and faster.

Churches are made up of people. The people in your pews are no different than those involved in the activities described above. We are in the information age and have more tools at our disposal than ever. This communication revolution has also impacted the way organizations are funding their budgets. In 2008, organizations like The Salvation Army began accepting donations via text messaging. Later that same year, this same organization—an organization that is more than one hundred years old—built Red Kettle widgets that anyone could include on their blog or Facebook page to remind those in their social network of the opportunity to give back to others in need. This multiplied the collection efforts by leveraging the social networks of their donor base.

Perhaps the last front of this revolution is the church, which is notorious for resisting change on all fronts. As the people in our pews are being shaped by the culture we live in and the mediums by which we communicate, we as church leaders can either bury our heads in the sand or embrace the new technology and use it to our advantage. The rules of engagement have changed. The church member is driving the funding and decision making of our churches. It's only a matter of time before every church leader admits it and begins to strategically think about how to use this revolution to the benefit of the ministry of the church.

The Pulpit vs. the Pew on Tithing

What we have found to be particularly interesting when it comes to the topic of tithing and church giving is the great divide that exists between formal statements from denominations and the people who collectively comprise our local churches. It seems that every denomination has a conservative, traditional stance on the issue. But that message is not so clear from the pulpit and even less clear in the mind and practice of the person in the pew.

If we take a step back from the situation, the issue becomes clear. And it has nothing to do with theology. Churches for centuries have commanded their members to give to support the ministry of the church. For the most part, congregants responded in turn. The primary question that church members have been asking is, "How?" *How do I give my time, talent, and money?* But that question has changed.

> A new generation is nonresponsive to the assumption made by church leaders that if you are a church member, then you will tithe.

The first question is not "How can I give?" but "Why should I give to you?" A new generation is nonresponsive to the assumption made by church leaders that if you are a church member, then you will tithe. And church leaders are foolish to expect people to tithe "just because." That line is only reserved for parents. (And even in that scenario, it rarely works.)

In this chapter, we will consider how this conversation is changing and what implications it has upon funding and sustaining the ministry of the local church.

35

The Heart of the Issue

The heart of this issue lies in the options church members have available to them. There was a time when the church was the most obvious place for charitable donations because of the commitment the church carried to provide local, social-based ministry as well as global endeavors. Outside the church, there were very few options available.

Over time this has changed. People now have to decide not just between one or two options but among a seemingly unlimited number of choices and organizations to which to donate. While the church had been doing this very well for centuries, other organizations have been perfecting the work of raising funds, too. Now other nonprofits are paying attention to what churches are doing to attract people and raise funds. It's time for churches to begin paying close attention to successful nonprofits.

When people have choices, they struggle to make the right choice. Barry Schwartz contends in his book *The Paradox of Choice* that consumers think more options will lead to a greater sense of satisfaction. The opposite is true. More options actually create an equal amount of anxiety when it comes to decision making for fear of making the wrong decision.

Think about this concept from the perspective of the person in the pew. If he or she only has a limited number of dollars to donate, it can become an overwhelming task for that person to decide where that money should go. This puts the church in a position that for the most part it has avoided up to this point in history. The position is this: every church must now justify to its members and regular attenders why they should donate their limited funds to this particular church.

After the fall of Enron and similar organizations, a whole new era of corporate compliancy and accountability was ushered in through government regulations to ensure the circumstances that led to Enron's demise and the devastation of its employees and shareholders would be avoided at all costs. The call for increased transparency and accountability was unexpectedly directed at churches, too. Many people who see their pastors and staff members driving nicer cars and living in nicer neighborhoods than they could ever dream of affording themselves struggle to adopt the worldview that they must give their tithe to the church. So these people respond in silence to the pleas from the pulpit to give, give, give.

Perhaps some have decided that the church already has enough so they choose to donate their money where the greatest need is clearly articulated. And you should know that we're not against pastors being compensated fairly for their work and expertise. The pastor is given great responsibility and is asked to lead very complex organizations. It is a job that rarely offers a break and demands the pastor be on call around the clock. Taking into account the perception of some of the people who sit in our pews is important as we shape our strategy moving forward.

We suppose some pastors would object to the idea of having to justify why their members should give. Many might continue to carry forward the "just because" argument. The brutal facts tell us that—like it or not—church leaders have the responsibility to generate the contributions necessary to build the ministry of the church, even if that means entertaining the question "why?" The people in the pews have a virtually unlimited number of choices and options when it comes to giving their time, money, and talent. Why should they give it to your church?

> The people in the pews have a virtually unlimited number of choices and options when it comes to giving their time, money, and talent. Why should they give it to your church?

Exploring the Impact of *American Idol* on Church Giving

The next revolution in charitable giving may be companies allowing their customers or members to decide who they support through their philanthropic endeavors. Trip Advisor, an online travel information Web site, asked the public to decide which cause the company should support. Here is a summary of how the program worked: Trip Advisor offered five options for the public to choose from regarding how the $1 million pledge would be divided. Polls closed on a certain date, and then the results determined how the money was spent and which organizations and causes were supported.

We wonder what this might look like in church. What if the initial budget presentation to the church body signaled the opening of the polls where members could pledge their monetary gifts for the specific ministries they wanted to support? Then after a certain period, the polls would close and the results would be tallied. The end result would be any ministry that was significantly underfunded would be cut from the budget.

This works for *American Idol,* which is arguably the most successful talent-seeking competition in history. It has also produced multiple pop and country music stars who have been and continue to be very successful. The dark side of the process is that sometimes even the most talented get cut. This would also have to be considered within the church setting. It may mean that a long-standing ministry might end up subject to the proverbial axe.

The appeal for us (even as church leaders) is that it puts the power back in hands of the people in the pews—the ones who are giving the dollars to fund the budget. And people tend to be more committed and give more when they have a say in how their donations are used.

"They" Want to Know Your Church's Spending Habits

People want to know how the money they donate is being used. The Texas State Attorney General's Office recently launched an online tracking service to let interested people know how the charities they support are spending the money they receive. This program is indicative of the shift that is taking place and mirrors the level of transparency and accountability that the people in our pews are demanding.

We encourage church leaders not to see this shift as a demand that is being forced upon them. In fact, we see it as just the opposite. This new culture of organizational accountability offers church leadership the opportunity to involve the church's membership in the decision-making process and provides a mechanism whereby the donors can be involved in how the money they give is being spent.

Technology is changing everything. And it's not limited to how we communicate and collaborate. The social media revolution is returning the power back to the smallest common denominator, the individual donor. What if an independent source began tracking the spending habits of your church and publishing that information for everyone (i.e., the world) to review? Would your church's financial decisions stand the test of public scrutiny? Traditional nonprofits are already being watched closely by independent entities. It won't be long before churches will find themselves being tracked and watched in a similar way too.

Stewardship and Assimilation Are Closely Linked

A connection exists between those within your donor base who volunteer their time and talent in addition to their money and those who only offer a portion of their financial blessing. Those who volunteer with an organization naturally give at higher levels than those who simply provide donations to the cause.

There are four major segments when you consider the life cycle of a church member: acquisition, assimilation, retention, and attrition. The healthy church balances its acquisition strategy with an emphasis on assimilation, which results in long-term retention and minimizes premature attrition.

The assimilation stage is where we help new members or regular attenders find a small group or ministry area in which to invest and become personally involved. Church growth practice affirms that people who find a good fit in a small group setting also experience high levels of overall satisfaction, are more likely to volunteer and more likely to hold leadership positions, and give more consistently than members or regular attenders who remain wallflowers.

The better we are at getting our members and regular attenders involved, the better givers they will be. Why? Because giving is the result of emotional, relationship-driven experience. The best givers in your church also have the most invested emotionally. If this is true, then it makes sense that those who have the most invested in your church should also have a way to influence the direction of their organization from a fiscal and ministry perspective.

Giving and the Church Member Experience

We try to read as much as we can from many different sources. This exposes us to different ideas both inside and outside our discipline of stewardship and giving. We often find ourselves borrowing from other disciplines and incorporating them into our work. One such example can be found in Bruce Temkin's blog *Customer Experience Matters*.

Temkin's identified six "laws" that define the customer's experience. We immediately began thinking about how his laws could be translated into the vocabulary and culture of the church. Since church giving is an emotional process, the stronger the experience is with a local church, the more likely the individual is to contribute through his or her time, talent, and resources.

Here is our attempt to do just that:

The 6 Laws of Church Member Experience

1. Every ministry opportunity or worship service creates a personal reaction.

2. People are instinctively self-centered rather than corporate-centered.

3. Church member familiarity (with doctrine, people, educational and service opportunities, etc.) breeds unity and clarity of focus.

4. Unengaged church members don't create engaged church members.

5. Church members (just like the rest of us) do what is measured, incented, and celebrated.

6. Church members can't fake (or fabricate) sincerity of belief or commitment.

These six laws will help us determine how we as church leaders can work toward creating authentic experiences for our members that will foster and sustain a sense of internal connection with a local body of believers that motivates them to respond in measurable ways such as giving of their time, talents, and treasures. Knowing that giving is an emotional process, relationships become the catalyst to better giving and more sustained funding over time.

1. Every ministry opportunity or worship service creates a personal reaction. The temptation in this law is to assume that the church member is a customer who is shopping for a particular product. This temptation has monopolized the discussion of church growth and music style to the point that we've actually created a subgroup of people (church leaders and members) who shop church based on the style of music. (The fallacy of that premise and its unintended results are for another discussion.)

That's not how to interpret this law. In fact, it misses the point altogether. Every ministry opportunity, act of service, or worship that our church members participate in contributes to their total church experience in addition to the spiritual formation of their own lives. And that total church experience directly results in an inward connection that is either strengthened or weakened.

Keeping in mind that giving is an outward sign of an inward commitment to an idea, cause, or person that inspires or motivates an individual, the level of giving in our church is directly related to our ability to continue to contribute to a healthy and complete total church experience that fosters authentic encounters with God and results in true spiritual transformation.

Are we measuring the results or, as Jesus might have said, the fruit of our ministry to ensure that it's leading people to become followers of the Way, or is our ministry simply filling the to-do lists of well-intentioned, churchgoing people? The former experience is ripe to produce faithful and sustained giving while the latter will at best produce a token of affection.

2. Instinctively, people are self-centered much more than they are corporate-centered. Even though people gather in faith groups all around the world on, at least, a weekly basis, that doesn't mean they have a corporate-centered mentality. Finding an individual role within a larger context is what leads to those formative, relationship-building experiences that create a sense of ownership and belonging to a corporate entity. And giving is a natural response to feelings of ownership and belonging. In theological words, we might say "communion of the saints."

It is in serving together, living our lives together, praying together, etc. that we become aware that we are not lone rangers sent by God to save the world on our own. Rather, a healthy understanding would render a much different perspective, one that might be closer to the notes on the page of a scripted symphony rather than an impromptu guitar solo.

People give money when they realize they are part of a cause, entity, or organization that is larger than themselves. The paradox lies in attempting to foster a corporate mentality within our individualistic American culture.

3. Church member familiarity (with doctrine, people, educational and service opportunities, etc.) breeds unity and clarity of focus. The old saying in sales is that "people buy from who they know, like, and trust." The more familiar people are with your church, the values you represent, and the people who make up your church, the more likely they are to fund and support your ministry. What's difficult as church leaders (people who are in the middle of everything) is that not everyone is privy to the same amount (and depth) of information you have about your church. So we assume everyone just knows what we believe and the ministry and service opportunities available. We can't afford to make this assumption, and doing so will impact giving habits.

Those people who are most familiar with your church's theology and doctrine, operations, leadership, and overall ministry will be the ones who have the strongest emotional and identity connection with your church. This will result in faithful church member giving. Maybe it's time to begin hosting a coffee hour or small, arranged dinners with small groups of your people so that they can personally hear the heartbeat of every church leader.

4. Unengaged church members don't create engaged church members. People who are excited about your church and the ministry it provides will naturally draw people to your church. Word-of-mouth recommendations will always reign supreme in influencing people. In fact, your church members will consistently be more effective at generating new prospects and converting those prospects to new church members than church staff will ever be.

Rest assured, marginal or inactive church members will never do anything to generate interest in the ministry of your church. In fact, they may do more harm than good. (But that is another discussion for another time.) Engaged church members create an ideal environment to grow stewards, people who understand that all they have are assets entrusted to them to be managed ultimately for Kingdom growth.

> Rest assured, marginal or inactive church members will never do anything to generate interest in the ministry of your church.

5. Church members (just like the rest of us) do what is measured, incented, and celebrated. The hard part about this one is that church leaders are not naturally wired to quantify the ministry impact they are having. Church leaders are visionaries and dreamers. We are people who are much more comfortable with our rhetoric than our calculators.

The exception to this is the emerging role of the church business administrator or executive pastor roles that are being filled by business professionals gifted in the areas of accounting, human resources, administration, and business management. This is a good thing and should be viewed as a complement to the other ministry staff of the local church.

Even though quantifying ministry impact or ministry results is not natural, it doesn't absolve church leadership from producing these results for the larger congregation. After all, it's the people in the pews who put the dollars in the plate. They have a right to know the numbers and should have the final say in how the money of the church is being used.

Para-church and secular nonprofit leaders are doing a much better job at proving the effectiveness of every dollar contributed to their organization than the church. We need to step it up and be prepared to defend why the church is the best place to invest in Kingdom-building activities.

After the work has been done and the results are in, it's easy to celebrate the success and reflect on the failures. Measuring results, incenting performance, and celebrating successes emphasizes action rather than talk. And if there is one thing the church could benefit from, it's more action and less talk.

Bottom line, the people in the pews are evaluated based on their performance in their own jobs; they expect the same accountability to be extended to their church leaders. People will give more consistently and in greater amounts when they understand how their money is being used and see the results of the ministry their dollars fund.

6. Church members can't fake (or fabricate) sincerity of belief or commitment. If giving is an outward sign of an inward commitment, then consistent, generous giving is an indication of sincerity of belief in and commitment to your church. It's easy to find reasons not to give. And it's easy to fake a habit of giving but only for a period of time.

When you look at your giving records, do you see an increasing number of people consistently giving, a stagnant group of people consistently giving, or a decreasing number of people consistently giving?

If you're seeing an *increasing number* of consistent givers, congratulations! You're doing all the right things to communicate your message and get buy-in from your members who are in turn responding measurably with their financial support. No doubt you've also seen a rise in volunteerism and ministry activities.

If you're seeing a *stagnant group* of people, then you know that you're doing almost all of the right things. The part of your plan that's missing is the replication or multiplication of church members who are learning the habit of giving consistently.

This is where most churches are today. And there is little energy spent on creating new givers or growing stewards simply because churches are meeting their budgets and satisfying their expenses. But that's not enough. Such a perspective is also shortsighted since we know that replicating and multiplying givers creates more money for more ministry. The church doesn't have the option of saying "that's enough" until Christ returns.

If you're seeing a *decreasing number* of people consistently giving, it's time to face reality. There is a breakdown in your stewardship development strategy. Again, the tough part is that too often churches wait until the giving decreases measurably before they respond aggressively.

We can't emphasize enough that giving is just one measuring tool; it's interconnected with how excited your church members are about the ministry of your church, their willingness to volunteer and take on leadership roles, how they talk about the church to their friends and neighbors, etc. If you want to increase the ministry capacity of your church, focus on growing stewards—people who give of their time, talents, and treasures. This involves a holistic plan that will ultimately create balanced, healthy church members and will result in balanced, healthy church growth.

There is no detailed, step-by-step plan for you and your staff to follow that ensures you're providing space for your members to hear and see your vision, taste and feel the culture of the church, and decide whether or not your church is the place they want to participate in by giving their time, talents, and resources.

It really boils down to a "both-and" solution. As church leaders, we're responsible for providing spiritually formative, relationship-building opportunities for our members, regular attenders, and even our visitors. This function is vital to church health and fostering a sense of ownership by the congregation that brings with it a sense of personal responsibility and accountability. Such behavior and feelings ensure fully funded and long-term sustainable ministry both now and in the future.

The rest of the experience must be left with the working of the Holy Spirit in the lives of your people. At some point, we have to trust that God will inspire the hearts of people to give generously in response to his Gospel and those who claim to be followers of Jesus.

What Churches Can learn from Wikipedia

Wikipedia, the online, user-generated content encyclopedia that spurred the "wiki" revolution, set a goal to raise $6.2 million in 2008. Most of the total amount raised was in the last six months of the year, and nearly one-third was raised over eight days in early December. (Yes, as in December 2008 . . . the one that was right smack dab in the middle of this big problem called a recession.)

So what can churches learn from Wikipedia?

1. Wikipedia involves people in its work. The contemporary church model is designed to fund a small group of staff members to do the work "on behalf of" the membership. Wikipedia finds its appeal in user-generated content. Essentially, that means the user is generating content that other users will find helpful and will—for lack of a better word—use. This model is indicative of the great shift that is taking place where people are looking to peers as well as experts for information that they will compile and use to come to a conclusion on any number of topics. Just because you are an expert, that doesn't mean you will be trusted.

Church leaders tend to cut the church member out of the creative planning and decision-making processes. Often, church leaders just want members who will say yes to whatever they have determined is right. The people in your pews want to be more involved in every aspect of your church's ministry. They want a say in every level of decision making. And we know that the more involved people are in this part of the process, the more ownership they feel, which results in high levels of satisfaction and commitment.

2. *Wikipedia depends on small donations from large groups of people. Churches thrive off the faithful giving of a few.* During this campaign, 125,000 people contributed to the goal of $6.2. That's an average donation of $49.60 per person. Let's take just the 50,000 people who contributed during an eight-day rush in December 2008 to make up the remaining $2 million needed. That small group alone averaged only $40 per person.

What does all this mean? Stop looking for the big windfall. Start expanding your focus on growing stewards across a broader section of your membership. The problem is that we've hitched our funding models in churches to only 10–20 percent of our membership. That's dangerous and financially unstable.

3. *The founder made a personal appeal to Wikipedia's community. Church leaders have bought into the myth that their membership won't tolerate straight talk about contributions.* Imagine you are Jimmy Wales, founder of Wikipedia. You get a memo sometime around the end of November 2008 that says you are one-third away from your annual goal. What do you do? Panic. (That's probably what most of us would do.) But Jimmy didn't panic; he took advantage of the desperate situation to inspire generous giving among those who believed in what he was doing. He went to his audience and asked for their support, and they gave it to him.

Pastor, if you're like most of your peers, you were trained to cut expenses, pray, and hope for the best. None of that is inherently bad. But it's missing an important element. People give based on felt and perceived need. And the people who are most plugged in to what you're doing are statistically most likely to kick in a little extra when times are tough.

We can only imagine how many countless dollars fear has left on the table in churches all across the country. That means there is much necessary ministry that won't be accomplished because the funding won't be there. We're thrilled for Wikipedia. We only wish the headlines read that churches were as successful funding their ministry budgets too. Our work is of eternal importance.

The conversation has changed. The first question a church member asks is not "How can I give?" but "Why should I give?" and more important, "Why should I give to your church?" As the rate of nonprofits continues to outpace the creation and development of new churches, there are more people competing for the dollars of the people in your pews than ever. Church leaders will have to play by the new rules of engagement if they hope to continue to connect with their people and provide compelling reasons why they should fund the church and its mission efforts.

Increased demand for organizational transparency and accountability means that the church leader must give up a certain level of control. Church members want more than a business meeting. They want to see measurable results and feel confident that their money is being used to achieve maximum results. People want a say in how the money is being used. This is going to require a great deal of change, uncomfortable change, in order to develop a model and method that operates successfully within your church context.

> As the rate of non-profits continues to outpace the creation and development of new churches, there are more people competing for the dollars of the people in your pews than ever.

Stewardship education is considered by some church leaders as nonessential. No one will publicly admit this, but judging by the lack of emphasis on stewardship education in our churches today, we see a much different story. The job of the church leader is to satisfy the needs of today and provide for ministry viability moving forward. What you refuse to change today may impact your church's ability to fully fund the ministry it will be given to do ten or twenty years from now.

DISCUSSION QUESTIONS

1. Before people want to know *how* they can give, they first want to know *why* they should give. In fifty words or less, what would you tell them? (Write it down and memorize it.)

2. What other charitable organizations are your members currently supporting financially? Are they giving less to the church because of these other opportunities?

3. Would you feel comfortable if an independent source began tracking your church's spending habits and sharing them for all to see? Why or why not?

4. Looking over The 6 Laws of Church Member Experience, how can you create authentic experiences that foster and sustain a sense of internal connection with believers and motivate them to respond in measurable ways?

5. What impressed you about how Wikipedia operates? How can you incorporate some of their business philosophies into how your church operates and does ministry?

Chapter 4

+ + +

RESPONSIBILITY: WHAT YOU WISHED THEY HAD PREPARED YOU FOR IN SEMINARY

"Whether or not they admit it,
today's preachers know they have
to persuade and sell."
—JAMES HUDNUT-BEUMLER

If no one has told you yet, let us be the first to break the news to you: the responsibility of ensuring the funds are available to fulfill your church's budgetary commitments and provide for long-term sustainable ministry falls to the pastor. No one is going to take the fall for you if everything goes bad. No one is going to give you all the credit when your efforts have yielded an abundance of resources. Individuals who derive their income from an organization that is dependent upon the generous giving of its membership should be concerned with the topic of fund-raising.

Those who wish to be pastors for their entire working careers need to accept the fact that fund-raising comes with the calling. We understand that no one told you this when you raised your hand or walked an aisle and expressed that God had called you to ministry. And we're certain this reality was not thoroughly explored during any of the ninety or so hours it took to complete your seminary training. Nonetheless, the responsibility is still yours to fulfill.

Pastors who survive in this profession are ones who make peace with the fact that they are fund-raisers. The leader of any organization with the hope of initiating change within the community in which it exists is the best positioned to accomplish this task. It certainly doesn't mean you have to make a go of it alone. But, just like the children we raise, the people we lead listen closely and watch carefully. They will naturally assume your posture regarding money. If it's a negative one, then you will forever find yourself in survival mode, struggling to stay alive. If, however, you choose to embrace this function and use your position of influence to your advantage, you will create a sustainable funding model that will lead to fully funded budgets and long-term ministry impact.

Reconciling the Role of Faith and Fund-Raising

Every pastor lives in between the tension of more money and more ministry. This becomes the catalyst for the conversation on the pastor as fund-raiser. To dispel the myths and anxieties we private Americans sometimes have about money, let us give you some insight into the profession of fund-raising.

A professional fund-raiser is someone who must subscribe to his or her ability to affect change on two levels: one, a general interest in helping others affect change, and two, a belief in and identification with the values, goals, and work

> Fund-raising is essentially providing the fuel for an organization or individual to accomplish some goal or task that they believe will make the world a better place.

of the organization represented. Fund-raising is essentially providing the fuel for an organization or individual to accomplish some goal or task that they believe will make the world a better place. Because of it, organizations experience fully funded budgets and sustainable work efforts that ultimately ensure stable and lasting results. This knowledge alone provides enough strength in the weakest moments to keep pressing on, to make one more phone call, write one more letter, and host one more dinner.

Great fund-raisers—those who experience the highest degrees of success—believe in the organization or cause they represent. There is a sparkle in their eyes when they talk about the work at hand. There is an "X" or "IT" factor that translates on a gut level and transfers an energy beyond words, which generates a measurable response. Fund-raising and development work are comprehensive and holistic efforts. They require every skill imaginable, including a childlike belief that the impossible can take place.

The thought of asking people for money makes most pastors sweat and perhaps even have a number of physical and emotional reactions. When we take an honest look at the role and task of a professional fund-raiser, it's not so different from the role of the pastor. Further, we begin to understand why pastors are the best people to fulfill this function and lead this effort within the organization they serve.

Every Pastor Is a Fund-Raiser

Why does fund-raising lack that sense of "calling" that being a pastor carries with it? If fund-raising is simply a transaction, then we miss the point. Fund-raising is about providing a compelling vision that invites others to participate in and support with their time, talents, and treasures to bring about a change that is larger than any one single person, organization, or program can accomplish.

A passionate appeal from the leader of an organization or cause who refuses to believe that it's just about a monetary transaction between a wealthy individual and an organization that simply takes place to satisfy the needs of both parties finds the strength to carry out this responsibility by seeing how it fits within the larger picture of organizational health and financial viability. The task of asking people for money becomes the chance to invite others to participate in the work that you are doing. This is not so different from a pastor who participates in weekly visitations and community outreach or counsels a family as they are making a decision whether or not to move their church membership.

Pastors carry the burden of the greatest message and vision of all time, the Good News of the Gospel. The reality check is this: if you can't inspire someone to financially support the work of your church, maybe it's time to take a look in the mirror to ensure you believe what you're preaching.

Seven Things to Get You Motivated to Stop Talking and Get Moving

The hardest part about fulfilling your role as fund-raiser is in the doing. A friend who is a sales manager says it like this, "Sales is 90 percent behavior and 10 percent intellect." The conflict comes within the type of person who is generally called to pastor. There is nothing wrong with you, but you need to understand that most pastors are comfortable in the world of theory and philosophy. Conversely, most pastors are uncomfortable in the world of measurements, statistics, and benchmarks. Again, this tendency is not bad; it's what makes you great at what you do. What you need to understand is why you are naturally opposed to the idea of fund-raising. If you never ask anyone for money, you'll never get it.

Consider these the next time you find yourself tempted to sit back and hope the details and the necessary funding just magically come together:

1. It's never as bad as it seems, and it's never as good as it seems. This is some of the best advice received from a mentor long ago. It applies today. No matter how much money you need to raise or how far behind you are year to date, the situation as it is right now could be better and could be worse. The important first step is to state the obvious. It forces you to deal with reality and avoid a false sense of security.

2. *Difficult times weed out unqualified leaders.* We're not talking about education and degrees. Leadership requires guts. It requires faith. It requires an absolute trust that the organization will succeed. If you can't inspire yourself to believe, you won't inspire anyone else. One of the things you'll notice with toddlers is that they have not yet considered that there is something they can't do. Yes, they find themselves in trouble when they cross established boundaries, but that doesn't keep them from trying. It's inspiring to witness such childlike effort to reach for what is desired, no matter how impossible it may seem. Believe in the impossible; your membership is counting on you.

3. *Never stop learning.* Overwhelming situations are great. They force us to focus, learn, and think in new ways and to take risks. The most important task is to never stop learning, and we advise you to seek out books and people. What a great opportunity to call some prominent business leaders in your community, take them to lunch, and find out their opinion on the subject of asking for money. Chances are you'll shock the socks right off of them, make a new friend, gain some valuable advice, and maybe meet a new church prospect or uncover an opportunity to share your faith with an unbeliever.

4. *Talk about it.* Most pastors never talk about stewardship and giving. But avoiding the subject doesn't make it any less real. Difficult conversations come with the job. Just be honest and always do what's in the best interest of the church. It's absolutely essential that you surround yourself with people you can trust, especially people who you perceive to be influencers in the community. Every church has them. These are the people who others watch and listen to, and they will follow their lead. It's important to have them on your side. Involving those influencers in your conversations and in your thinking will give them a behind-the-scenes look at the complexity of your job, allow them to offer some advice, and gives you the opportunity to win their support.

5. *Pray about it.* Wear out the same kneeling bench you ask your members to use each week. Here is a hint: Stop talking. Start listening. God already knows how bad it is and all the specifics of your situation. It's your job to get in touch with his presence in the midst of uncertain times. You can't fulfill the mythic god-man role you play in your church without an authentic sense of God's presence in your own life.

6. *Act.* If there is one thing we are great at doing in the church, it is talking God's vision to death. We have an innate ability to talk ourselves out of what God has called us to do, and we do it in the name of Jesus. The bottom line is success rarely leads to failure, but failure often leads to success. Do something, please!

7. *Stop worrying about whether or not you'll have a job.*
If you allow this fear to occupy your mind, you'll create what psychologists call a self-fulfilling prophecy. Do your job. Live up to the calling to which you have been called and start leading. The church is in desperate need of pastors who will quit worrying about their careers and focus on building the ministry of the Kingdom in the churches and communities where they serve and live.

There is a phrase a fellow staff member once me (Ben) before I went into a very difficult meeting with some church members who were not very happy with me. He smiled and said, "Look it in the teeth, even if it bites back." As pastors and church leaders, we believe we are called by God. Yes, the same God who brought the world into existence, the same God who provided bread and manna for his children to eat, the same God who used a boy to slay a giant, the same God who conquered sin through the death of his only son. That same God called us to be representatives of those who survive and thrive in impossible situations, and we must believe and act upon our belief that God will provide and continue to be faithful as he has done time and again.

> The church is in desperate need of pastors who will quit worrying about their careers and focus on building the ministry of the Kingdom.

Five Steps to Ensure More Money for More Ministry

Let us provide a word of caution. These five steps outlined below are guiding principles, not a model for you to replicate within your own church. These steps will look different in every setting. What's important is that if you keep these principles close by as you develop your church strategy, you will cover the essential elements of achieving fully funded budgets and long-term sustainable ministry.

1. Establish a systematic strategy.

We don't want to spend a great deal of time on this step because there is an infinite amount of resources on building your church strategy. What we do want to advocate is that stewardship be one of the core elements included in your church plan. How are you going to educate and cultivate a generous culture? What ways will you provide for your members to contribute? Those kinds of questions will require you to make decisions about what you want to accomplish; it's those types of decisions that will lead to the results you are aiming to achieve.

Your strategy should exist on a leadership and church member level. Churches that have been the most successful at getting the money they need for the ministry they feel called to do establish an annual stewardship and giving strategy that is comprehensive in nature. In addition, each element is outlined and provides a road map to follow. Knowing where you want to end up is the first question you must answer before you begin your journey. One thing is for sure: if you're unsure about your plan, you'll certainly fail.

2. Start talking about it.

Communication theory tells us that ideas are not "real" until we speak them out loud. This is one reason verbal exchange is part of the human development process. Take the marriage relationship for example: successful marriages have open lines of communication. This is an intentional decision and doesn't just happen by accident. Marriages survive the test of time not because there is an absence of conflict. Rather, they survive because both partners have agreed to talk about the source of tension until it is resolved.

It's the same with tithing in the church. Talking about it makes it less scary and provides the opportunity to deal with objections from the pulpit and the pew. For too long churches have breezed through this subject buried inside new member materials when it should be incorporated into every aspect of the life of the believer. Are we suggesting that you always talk about tithing and ask for money? Absolutely not! What we *are* suggesting is that a biblical steward sees everything he or she has as a gift from God to be used for the advancement of the Kingdom. There is often a stark difference between this theological premise and the premise by which many of our church members (and leaders) live their lives. Assuming the posture of a biblical steward is the result of the work of the Spirit in the life of the believer, and this work is primarily fostered through spiritual formation and discipleship, which are primary functions of local church ministry; talking about it provides a way to fulfill this obligation.

This is the only way to overcome the assumptions many make about church giving. The more we ignore the subject, the more mysterious it becomes and the more removed we are from the truth on the subject. In a time when consumer debt has risen to unprecedented levels, the church risks being perceived as completely irrelevant if it has nothing to say on the subjects of biblical money management and stewardship. Those outside the church are spending every available resource to reach for the dollar of the person in your pew. All you have to do is take advantage of the opportunity you have to speak to your people on a regular basis.

3. Set expectations.

Tell your church from the beginning that you don't pay the light bill with a note of prayer. People need to remember that it takes money to operate any organization. Believe it or not, the people in the pews are very busy. And even though you give them a monthly operational budget to review, it's easy to forget the daily needs of operating the church. It's important that people are reminded that just like it takes money to operate a home, the church needs money to operate too.

If you're not comfortable talking to the chairman of your trustees, finance committee, deacons, or stewardship committee, it's time to get up close and personal. They need to know that you are furiously trying to understand how to provide for the fiscal health of the church; they also need to hear your heart and passion. There is a balance between the two that you and those in lay leadership must find. When you do achieve it, it's absolutely dynamite.

As expectations rise for churches to provide programs to meet the complex needs of the community, those programs will have an expense associated with them. Quantify those costs and justify them. If the program doesn't warrant the investment, then don't do it. If it does, then your people will understand the fiscal investment necessary to launch and sustain this new program or ministry. Another undervalued area is church assimilation programs. Set expectations with new members that you expect them to contribute their time, money, and talents. And then explain why. Be sure you can explain the "how" and the "why."

4. Make the ask.

Make the ask is the fund-raising equivalent of bring the tithe. Focusing on this step means providing ways for your members to financially contribute to your organization. Just as a healthy business has more than one stream of income, your church should offer multiple ways for your membership to contribute.

Give people ways to contribute and teach them how to use those tools. Some of the most common ways are: weekly offering envelopes, electronic giving, special offerings, major gifts, and planned giving or bequests.

Offering Envelopes. Offering envelopes are the most proven method used by churches to generate and deliver the contributions necessary to do the work of the church. There is a reason why our secular and parachurch nonprofit brothers and sisters spend money executing donor campaigns using envelopes. It's not because they think envelopes are cool. They use them because they work, and they deliver the funds necessary to operate their organization and support the cause for which they exist.

Electronic Giving. Electronic giving methods are simply another option to provide your membership to support your church. There are many companies that can give your church this functionality without the worry of administering the funds and negotiating contracts with banks and credit card companies. Most electronic giving programs also allow the church to make a decision regarding the use of credit cards. As the consistency of regular attenders continues to decline, church giving via bank drafts or collecting money for special events via your church's Web site makes it easy for your members to participate and your staff to administrate.

Special Offerings. Designing custom offering envelopes is easy and costs little more than the stock offering envelopes you may be purchasing today. This gives you the freedom to create a special envelope that is designed in such a way to visually express the brand of the campaign. It also highlights the importance of this offering to the overall mission of the church and offers church leaders an easy way to point out the causes and work the members' funds are supporting.

Contribution Statements. This was once shared by a very wise man: "Everyone likes to keep score." Contribution statements hold us accountable to our commitment to support the ministry of the local church. Those churches that use these regularly notice an impact on giving. These are an essential tool for any church or Christian ministry. Isn't it interesting that when we know we owe money for a service or product we ask them to send us an invoice before we pay them? The people who sit in our pews are no different.

Major Gifts. These can come in many forms such as cash or stock transfers. These types of gifts are not only large in sum but are also usually tied to a specific event, fund, or purpose. This is where pastors must leverage their position to identify those within the membership who have the ability to give in this way and to share the details of the vision and plan in a way that inspires the giving of these members. People will support those organizations and causes that they believe in and that help them feel as if they are contributing to something larger than what they could accomplish on their own.

Planned Giving or Bequests. Colleges and universities have been doing this for a long time. Often these funds are included in a total endowment fund that is invested, and the interest is used to provide any necessary funding. This concept is quickly finding its way into funding models of churches under the title of estate tithing. This is when people write in their wills that a portion of their estate is dedicated to a specific church or organization. It's an easy process for the church and the church member. The impact of large gifts like this can truly make a difference.

Every church leader should consider how these and other methods of giving can contribute to a sustainable funding model that will propel the church toward questions of "What's next?" instead of "What now?" The most successful organizations at generating contributions for the ministry of the church are not afraid to make the ask. Even Jesus thought asking was important. Why should we think any differently?

5. Report the results.

As church leaders, we are responsible for taking the pains necessary to report the effectiveness of the ministry of the church. This directly speaks to the principles of accountability. Every organization should be examining every program or effort funded to ensure that it's the best use of the funds. When you consider the nonprofit world, one that exists on the donations of its members or the public, it's absolutely essential to prove that the money donated accomplishes the advertised goal.

Why is this so important? Because the people in your pews don't have to give to you. We know that they have money to give. We also know that a majority of charitable giving in the U.S. is made through religious organizations. And every day new opportunities arise and present themselves to the people in your pews. So why should they give to you instead of someone else? (Again, the "just because" argument doesn't work.)

> Every day new opportunities arise and present themselves to the people in your pews. So why should they give to you instead of someone else?

This can be done through annual reports, testimonies, bulletin inserts, goal boards, etc. Get creative, but know that people expect results.

In the end, the responsibility to teach stewardship, giving, and, more important, tithing falls upon the leaders of the church. That means being unsuccessful in this area is a direct result of our efforts. Those of us who have been given the responsibility of managing the affairs of a local church have a lot on us, but that doesn't absolve us from the responsibility of stewardship and giving. Perhaps we should re-evaluate where we are spending our time and our teaching. If we have no plan, we can't blame anyone but ourselves when we don't like the results.

Develop a Church Giving Plan . . .
Without the Pastor

Is there anything church leaders can do to ensure that the necessary money is available to continue the ministry of the church without senior leadership? It will always be easier to raise money or increase church giving when stable, senior church leadership exists, particularly when that senior leadership has the support and trust of the congregation. But what happens when the situation is less than perfect?

Perhaps we could consider treating this scenario just like we do our own investment portfolios—with a plan. More often than not, stewardship education is only invoked and the stewardship committee active when building projects are in progress. Such behavior and thinking is shortsighted. Without senior leadership, stewardship committees should be shouldering the responsibility of working with the church staff to develop a holistic plan that speaks to the continuation and growth in church giving no matter the circumstances.

We suspect that the hard work it will take on the front end to put together a comprehensive church giving plan will be worth the effort and will ensure that the ministry of the church continues with or without senior leadership. A plan provides a written explanation that forces conversation and commitment and serves as a measuring tool to direct our energy toward accomplishing the goals we defined.

Stewardship Involves
Responsibility and Accountability

Stewardship carries with it a sense of responsibility, a sense that God has given us the time, talents, and money we have for a reason. He expects us to find a way to use or spend those resources in such a way that it impacts the lives of others, especially the marginal members of society. This is not a responsibility that comes from a sense of fear, a fear that God will punish us if we don't do anything with what he has entrusted to us. This responsibility, rather, comes from a sense of gratitude in light of the sacrifice that Jesus made for us on the cross. Before we can bring value to the concept of stewardship, we must be mindful of the responsibility and accountability that we as church leaders accept when we respond to the call of God to lead in local church ministry.

DISCUSSION QUESTIONS

1. When did you discover that your role as pastor included the responsibility of fund-raising? (If it was just after reading this chapter, how does that make you feel?)

2. What motivation do you need to stop talking and get moving when it comes to fund-raising? (Look over the list of seven in this chapter to get you started.)

3. Look over the Five Steps to Ensure More Money for More Ministry in this chapter. Which of these guiding principles spoke to you the most? Why?

4. Are you making "the ask" in multiple ways? Once members know *why* they are giving, they want to know *how* they can give—and different people want to give in different ways. What avenue for giving do you need to add right now?

5. If, for some reason, your church were to have a different pastor a month from now, would giving decline? How can you ensure that ministry is funded regardless of the leadership?

Chapter 5

+ + +

TRANSFORMATION: WHY HOPE IS NOT A STRATEGY

"Therefore, for the Christian,
proper management of money and possessions
grows out of an understanding of the biblical
principles of financial stewardship."
—ROD ROGERS

Hope is not a strategy. That sentence always rings true during difficult situations, and we encourage you to repeat it to others as an encouragement to develop and work a plan when an impossible task is at hand. The same is true when it comes to the topic of church giving. Too many times we allow stewardship to become less than what it should be in our planning, preparation, and execution of our responsibilities to manage the affairs of a local church.

Don't you just love the imagery Paul uses in first few verses of Romans 12 when he talks about being changed forever? The word for transformation is grounded in our understanding of metamorphosis, which brings with it a sense of external and internal change. Transformation signifies a revolutionary process that leaves the subject of the metamorphosis different and unable to return to its previous state.

Topics of spiritual formation and discipleship seem to be the closest to this understanding. We also suggest that you view stewardship as equal to discipleship. A steward is someone who is entrusted with the wealth and power of someone else and given authority to act on his or her behalf with that wealth and power. When we confess Jesus Christ as our Lord and Savior, we have restored Jesus as owner of all that we have—our time, talent, and treasures—and we now are entrusted with those resources to replicate in others what has happened in our own lives.

Gandhi said, "If more Christians were like their Christ, the whole world would be Christian." We're convinced that the first place people outside the faith look for credibility and substance is within the personal lives of those who profess to be followers of Christ. If a total transformation has not taken place, then there is little reason for the individual to continue to pursue this path. When we equate stewardship with discipleship, we begin to see that it is so much more than just our money or another building campaign; it's a way of life that provides a discipline through which we practice our belief that all we have and are comes from God and is to be invested for eternal results.

How We Talk About Stewardship Matters

Therapists and professional counselors will tell you that *what* people say is less important than *how* they say it. Also, what they are *not* saying is quite telling. Using the word *stewardship* evokes many different emotions.

It definitely lacks the sense of appeal that *worship* or *preaching* or *Bible study* brings to the ear of many church leaders. We go to countless conferences to learn how to be better leaders, cast clearer visions, and more precisely capture the attention and minds of those inside and outside the church.

If we believe that *stewardship* is another word for *discipleship*, then we must begin to expect ourselves and all people of faith to practice this discipline. While rhetoric doesn't cause revolution, it certainly inspires others to consider a change. As church leaders, it is our responsibility to uphold the principles of stewardship not only within our own lives but within the life of the church. If the only time a person hears about stewardship is during a capital campaign or the annual "prove the tithe" emphasis, we have failed and left the people in our pews with little to combat the never-ending assault of appeals for their time, talent, and treasure from the world around us.

Too Important to Ignore

Stewardship may be an old word, but it doesn't make it any less relevant. In times of easy money, stewardship is a relaxed discipline. But in tough times, it seems to rise to the top. Growing stewards ensures you are growing healthy churches and providing for the ministry God has designed you to accomplish.

Church health is an important topic when you consider the complexity of an organization such as the church. With the demand for increased volunteers, programs, leadership, and money, it's a wonder how any church leader is able to keep pace with demand. This is why it's important to evaluate the health of your church.

We're consistently surprised at how few church leaders approach the subject of stewardship with a sense of urgency. We suspect most are dealing with the tyranny of the urgent instead of establishing an intentional strategy moving forward. Another force that we believe is working against this larger conversation is that most people only respond to pain, that which causes us to reconsider our current approach to the given set of circumstances that is consistently unable to correct the unavoidable discord between what is and what is desired.

> Where the people in the pews place their dollars demonstrates what they believe about the church's ability to accomplish the ministry that most directly occupies their thoughts and prayers.

Many churches have fully funded budgets. The levels of contributions today are enough to sustain their current ministry needs. We believe our responsibility is not only to ensure that ministry is fully funded today but also sustained over a long period of time. If this describes your situation, then you need to do two things: celebrate and prepare. You should celebrate God's provision and prepare for a season of limited resources.

Most complex organizations understand that sustainability is one of the key ingredients to long-term success. The church may be the most complex organization to ever exist, yet it's also the least likely to be concerned with sustainability. What does all of this have to do with stewardship and giving? Money offers churches the ability to accomplish the ministry God has called them to do.

Where the people in the pews place their dollars demonstrates what they believe about the church's ability to accomplish the ministry that most directly occupies their thoughts and prayers. If that place isn't the church, then we as church leaders must take a step back and evaluate the places of ministry we've decided to invest in to ensure that they match what God has placed on the hearts of the people in the pews. Unfortunately, most church leaders are highly trained speakers, not listeners. This makes the practice of listening problematic.

The irony is that what the people in the pews are asking of church leaders is often the very thing church leaders are asking of the people in the pews. Maybe it's time we start listening to each other.

Life Cycle of Church Membership As a Model for Growing Stewards

As you evaluate your people, programs, and giving, you will need to consider what systems and processes are in place to ensure that you are multiplying your efforts. Building on the discussion of the life cycle of church membership in chapter 3, a healthy church grows through executing four critical stages: acquisition, assimilation, retention, and attrition. Each stage is important when building a culture of generosity and fostering the characteristics of good stewards. This must be accomplished in a systematic way from an organizational perspective for your effort to have a lasting impact.

Let us briefly walk you through each stage:

Acquisition is the process of gaining new members. It's important to continually grow your base of potential givers of time, talent, and treasure if you hope to manage the ever-increasing demand of more ministry. The discipline of being a steward is great. Not every believer is willing to make the commitment to become a steward, so we can't expect every new member to become our next ministry leader, strategic planner, or faithful giver. We must always be looking to involve new people in our work, and what we are doing should be inspiring others to join and participate.

Assimilation is the process of involving those members in the work and ministry of your church. We know that those members who feel like they are contributing and know they have a place where they belong and are needed are going to exhibit and carry with them a greater sense of satisfaction with respect to your church and its ministry. This is key to establishing an emotional connection that must occur before someone will become a faithful, generous giver.

Retention is a critical stage, the most important when you consider the idea of sustainability. Gaining new people and incorporating them into your church is a time-consuming process. If a member doesn't stay very long, you don't get any return on your investment. It's only over time that you begin to see dividends on all your efforts. The longer members find themselves in this section of the life cycle, the more they will be able to multiply your efforts and inspire others to become stewards.

Finally, we move to *attrition*. Change is going to happen. This is what makes hanging your funding model on just 10 or 20 percent of your congregation so risky and dangerous. Attrition happens for many reasons: job changes or transfers, death, family circumstances, or disagreement with the direction of decision making of the church. Whatever the reason, it's clearly unavoidable, and church leaders should count on it. If your acquisition rate doesn't outpace your rate of attrition, you will experience negative growth, which will ultimately dry your well of resources and will hinder you from actualizing all the potential God has given you to develop and use.

No Plan Means More of the Same

The stages described above must be a part of your strategic plan to ensure you are building a model that supports the demands of more money and more ministry. No plan means more of the same. Don't expect things to change if you don't have a plan. Having a plan not only ensures the essential tasks are completed, it gives you something by which to measure your success. It's not easy work, but having a plan often eliminates surprises. The funding of your church should never be a surprise to the pastor.

Have you ever heard of a church requiring its staff to sign a contract? We have. It wasn't an employment contract, though refusal to sign it might have brought up such a conversation. The contract was intended to ensure that each member of the church leadership team understood and agreed to the same goals. It does no good to have a team of well-qualified staff members who don't operate as a team. It will translate into a division of interest among the greater church body and will disrupt your ability to build a sustainable model for your church.

Signing a contract is a scary thing for some. We encourage you to consider what a contract can do for you. It forces you as the pastor to carefully outline your goals and objectives for a specific period of time as well as outline your plan to achieve those goals. Then, the contract shares that information with those you depend on to help you achieve those goals. This should cause them to pause and consider if what they are doing is supporting the direction you're headed. It also offers every staff member a chance to ask questions or provide feedback that may or may not result in revising your goals and objectives. Once all the conversations are complete, you can focus on execution and measuring the results. It's impossible to know where you are unless you know where you are going.

Giving Is an Outward Sign of an Inward Commitment

A giving problem is first a spiritual problem. Much like baptism, the beginning of a generous heart begins within us and what we believe about our generous God. If all we have and are is ours, then we decide what God deserves based on our perceived value. If all we have and are is God's, then giving it back is a natural response made with a spirit of gratitude.

Generosity begins with the pastor. Your congregation is watching to see what type of lifestyle habits you are exhibiting in your own life. We suspect the reason so many pastors fail to preach and teach about the topics of stewardship and giving is because they know they are not being good stewards of the life they have been given. They aren't taking care of their bodies, spiritual life, family, or money. If you want to inspire your church to become generous people, it must begin within the life of the person in the pulpit.

> If you want to inspire your church to become generous people, it must begin within the life of the person in the pulpit.

Assume the Role of a Nonprofit Manager

We can't say enough about this challenge. If this is a new concept for you, you need to know that learning how to function as an executive director of the organization you lead is as much of a process as is becoming a great communicator. It requires knowledge and practice and must be cultivated over time. We suggest that you read books on nonprofit management and fund-raising. Consider meeting with development specialists at local colleges and universities. Offer to take financial managers to lunch and learn from them. Reading commentaries is good and leadership books are important, but avoiding the reality that the pastor is called to be a nonprofit manager and a shepherd is to avoid part of the calling.

Develop this practice in your life. We can almost guarantee that anyone you talk to—be it in person, over the phone, or via e-mail—will not turn your request down. To make things simple, just ask these four questions within the context of business management: What decisions led you to where you are today? What do you like most about what you do? What do you like least about what you do? Knowing what you know now, what would you tell yourself if you could when you were just beginning? People love to talk about themselves and their success. Listening to their stories will give you some fantastic ideas and possibly begin a new friendship. It's easy to meet with other pastors, but it's essential to get out of your comfort zone if you wish to learn new things and develop new habits.

Sustainable Funding Is Complex and Comprehensive

A long-term sustainable funding model requires a complex and comprehensive approach that will involve every aspect of your church's leadership, ministry, and membership. This book was never designed to answer all your questions or certify you as an expert. Its intent was to expose you to those core concepts that will serve as guiding principles on your journey toward a more sustainable ministry. If you've made it this far, then you have an idea that any effort to move in this direction will require people, planning, and a mix of hard work and determination.

Stewardship is hard work; it requires commitment, sacrifice, and discipline. Not everyone will be willing to go down this road. Those who aren't willing to go down this road with you aren't bad people; they are just not at the same point in their journey as you. It's important to know, especially when it comes to staff members and lay leaders, who is willing to practice the discipline of stewardship. Transforming your church and your church giving will require that you surround yourself with people who are committed to the same things you feel are important.

Invest in Our Children

Pastors will be measured not only by success during their tenure but by the legacy they leave behind. Both of us consider the impact our decisions will have on our families. The same should be true in the body of Christ. We are deeply concerned that pastors and teachers are not spending the time, effort, and energy necessary to cultivate generosity in the hearts, minds, and lives of the children in our churches. These little ones will learn from us, so we hope that you see the paramount importance of teaching what it means to be a steward to those who will lead our churches in the near future.

A legacy is not defined until someone is able to look back and draw the lines between the efforts of the past to the benefits of today. You may be in a church today where the tension of money and ministry are not a concern. We challenge you to consider what your church will look like in five, ten, or twenty years.

> Will there be enough money to meet the ministry demands of tomorrow? Will the babies you dedicate today be able to worship in the same church under the same name in fifteen years?

Will there be enough money to meet the ministry demands of tomorrow? Will the babies you dedicate today be able to worship in the same church under the same name in fifteen years? This is not someone else's problem; the answer to those questions depends upon what you do today.

Transformation Begins Within Us

Transformation is permanent and irreversible. Those who are brave enough to surrender all we have and are to the source of all our gifts will find a depth of experience and satisfaction that we often exchange for much less through our pursuit of pleasure and the perception of others. Those pastors who are courageous enough to scale stewardship within their own lives and the organizations they lead will experience more money, talent, and volunteers—all the elements necessary to do more ministry.

It's easy for us to get caught up in the churches we serve and forget that one church is one moving part of a much larger engine. The local church is the most important investment we make as leaders and as believers. We must do everything within our power to ensure the resources exist to support our work until Christ returns. We believe you can.

DISCUSSION QUESTIONS

1. Have you ever simply hoped for, or wished for, change? How did that work out? If hope is such a terrible strategy, why do so many pastors and leaders subscribe to it?

2. Do you believe that *stewardship* is another word for *discipleship*? If so, how can you move believers to practice this discipline more often and in greater ways?

3. As a pastor, you are a trained speaker but probably not a trained listener. What are the people in the pews telling you by their giving habits? How can you better hear each other?

4. Since generosity begins with the pastor, what does your congregation see in your lifestyle and giving habits? Do they see you putting your money where your mouth is?

5. What will your church look like five, ten, or twenty years from now? What are you doing to ensure that younger generations become the generous givers that will carry on the church's ministry?

Conclusion

We are so glad you made it through this book. We know it wasn't easy, and we're sure there were times when what we said made you upset or angry. You probably yelled a little; maybe even considered just throwing this book away. But there was something you read that made you want to continue. We're proud of you.

Making it through this book doesn't mean you've conquered the subject of stewardship and giving any more than writing this book has made us experts. We've simply started a dialogue that we want to see take place in a much larger context and with greater intensity than currently is the case. The conversations that led us to explore this subject in detail were had one-on-one in restaurants, airports, and coffee shops. It became apparent to us that while so many were pondering the same questions, few were brave enough to seek out others and work through their own frustrations.

Our understanding of stewardship came in the trenches, too, just like you. God provided a way for us to work with churches in the area of stewardship and giving while also serving churches in our own communities. We never expected to find a world of opportunity and an overwhelming sense of need. The more pastors we meet, the more we are convinced that with the right strategy and tools, all pastors have the ability to lead their church to achieve fully funded budgets and long-term sustainable ministry.

We may not know your name, the name of your church, or even the details of your current ministry situation, but know that we are praying for you. The church is the most important vehicle God gave us to continue the earthly ministry of Christ until his ultimate return; it is our best shot at fulfilling the Great Commission. It's too important of a task to let fail, as if failure were even an option. We must succeed, and with the blessing of God we will succeed.

31 STEPS
TO BETTER CHURCH GIVING

1. Be committed to asking the following two questions:
   - Are the stewardship practices of my church producing the results I/we desire?
   - What are the results I desire?

2. Develop a written theology of stewardship for your church. What does your church believe the Bible teaches about stewardship?

3. Understand that stewardship is about spiritual matters before it is about financial responses/investments:
   - It is about the heart.
   - My faith and my finances are connected.

4. Embrace stewardship as an identity rather than an activity.

5. Embrace giving as an act of worship.

6. Before the offering is received, share a brief story about how the congregation's giving is changing lives.

7. Celebrate transformational moments (with testimonies).

8. Move past a fear of talking about money at church.

9. Make sure that your personal financial affairs are congruent with how you are asking your people to behave:
   • Model generosity.
   • Model responsible financial strategies.

10. Take a long-term, holistic approach to creating a generous church.

11. Make your annual/operational planning process vision-driven.

12. Make sure those in financial decision-making roles (budget/finance) are committed to generosity.

13. Illustrate your annual spending plan:
   • Show people where their money is being spent.
   • Show people how their giving is changing lives.

14. Change the language of stewardship (if you want to change a culture, you begin by changing the language).
   • Giving *through* the church/budget as opposed to giving *to* the church/budget.

15. Rename your annual giving process using terms such as:
    - *MAP (Ministry Action Plan)*
    - *Compelled*
    - *Changing Lives*

16. Provide teaching/instruction around personal money management.

17. Develop a ministry to those God has given the capacity to make impact gifts (major donors).

18. Draw your core leadership group into the conversation around generosity.

19. Provide opportunities for your church to "practice" generosity (special offerings).

20. Integrate stewardship beliefs and expectations into your new member classes

21. Provide very practical ways for your people to "grow in the grace of giving."

22. Provide on a regular basis stewardship curriculum for your small groups.

23. Integrate some concept of stewardship in every teaching/preaching series.

24. Connect the giving of your people to transformation and life-change (testimony/life stories).

25. If debt service is being carried in the operational plan, consider a debt campaign.

26. Provide opportunity for your members to leave a "Legacy Gift" to your church through a planned-giving program.

27. Identify and thank all first-time givers.

28. Study and understand the generational differences in giving.

29. See the episodic capital campaign as a way to focus vision, grow discipleship, build unity, and raise significant resources without competing for operational dollars.

30. Do a stewardship assessment/audit with your church staff and leadership.

31. Become a life-long student of stewardship (see Further Reading section for suggested materials).

Further Reading

You need to know that this list is growing every day; we read a crazy number of books on a variety of subjects. There are more books that should be on this list, but we haven't read them all. We're sure there are a few we have read and unintentionally left off. Our intent is to provide a starting point rather than an exhaustive list.

Nonprofit Management

ROI for Nonprofits: The New Key to Sustainability by Tom Ralser

Good to Great by Jim Collins

Passing the Plate: Why American Christians Don't Give Away More Money by Christian Smith, Michael O. Emerson, and Patricia Snell

Tribes: We Need You to Lead Us by Seth Godin

Fund-Raising

The Ask: How to Ask Anyone for Any Amount for Any Purpose by Laura Fredricks

The Complete Guide to Fundraising Management by Stanley Weinstein

The 11 Questions Every Donors Asks: How You Can Inspire Someone to Give Generously by Harvey McKinnon

Ask Without Fear!: A Simple Guide to Connecting Donors with What Matters to Them Most by Mark A. Pitman

Biblical Stewardship

Making Change: A Transformational Guide to Christian Money Management by Ken Hemphill

Pastor Driven Stewardship: 10 Steps to Lead Your Church to Biblical Giving by Rod Rogers

Generosity: Moving Toward Life That is Truly Life by Gordon MacDonald and Patrick Johnson

New Day New Testament from Holman Bible Outreach International

The Eternity Portfolio: A Practical Guide to Investing Your Money for Ultimate Results by Alan Gotthardt

Raising More Than Money: Redefining Generosity Reflecting God's Heart by Doug M. Carter

In Pursuit of the Almighty's Dollar by Dr. James David Hudnut-Beumler

Technology and Giving

Digital Giving: How Technology is Changing Charity by Richard C. McPherson

People to People Fundraising: Social Networking and Web 2.0 for Charities by Ted Hart, James M. Greenfield, and Sherrax D. Haji

Chapter Quote References

Chapter 1: Michael O. Emerson and Christian Smith, *Passing the Plate* (New York: Oxford University Press, 2008), 29

Chapter 2: Tom Ralser, *ROI for Nonprofits* (Hoboken: John Wiley & Sons, 2007), 8.

Chapter 3: George Barna, *How to Increase Giving in Your Church* (Ventura: Regal Books, 1997), 62.3

Chapter 4: James Hudnut-Beumler, *In Pursuit of the Almighty's Dollar* (University of North Carolina Press, 2007), 230.

Chapter 5: Rod Rogers, *Pastor Driven Stewardship* (Dallas: Brown Books Publishing, 2006), 48.

About the Authors

Joel Mikell is president of RSI. With more than 25 years of local church ministry experience, he brings a passion for helping churches cast their vision to reach people for Christ, as only a pastor can. He has helped church leaders raise more than $500 million for Kingdom projects and has had the privilege of working with some of the most well-known churches and church leaders across the country. Joel and his wife, Donna, live in the Shelby, North Carolina, area.

Ben Stroup is a writer, blogger at BenStroup.com, and consultant who helps individuals and organizations navigate the new rules of conversation to achieve maximum impact through content strategy. He is an advocate for compelling content in a post-paragraph world and believes meaningful conversations are the most prized and coveted assets of one-person consulting firms, international charitable organizations, and multibillion dollar enterprises. Ben, his wife, Brooke, and their two sons, Carter and Caden, live in the Nashville, Tennessee, area.

Free Resources from RSI

WHAT YOU
DON'T KNOW
ABOUT YOUR
CHURCH CAN KILL
YOUR MINISTRY
POTENTIAL

rsi
Stewardship

www.rsistewardship.com/stewardship-resources

Free Resources from RSI

www.rsistewardship.com/stewardship-resources

Free Resources from RSI

Five Easy Ways for You to Connect with RSI

www.rsistewardship.com

1. Follow RSI on Twitter (@rsi_church) and Facebook (RSI Church Stewardship).

2. Download Joel Mikell's FREE *Debt Campaigns Can Work!* white paper (www.rsistewardship.com /stewardship-resources).

3. Sign up for RSI's e-newsletter.

4. Call RSI at 1.800.527.6824.

5. Contact RSI to discuss your church's needs.

Made in the USA
Middletown, DE
27 March 2015